"This book is a long-expected and theologic
future planters and existing pastors to con
starting churches by taking care of souls. I
passionate thoughts that make you value the godly and the biblical before the
trendy and the flashy. I can personally attest that Knight's teachings and stories
mentioned here are not only real but heartfelt, as I've personally benefited
from his living example and his pastoral leadership to treasure Jesus above
everyone and everything. I hope you can also be encouraged to do so as you
read this masterpiece."

Alejandro Molero, Pastor, Iglesia Biblica Sublime Gracia,
Washington, DC

"If you want to 'pastor-plant' a church that can be explained only in terms
of the power of the gospel at work, and if you want to plant a church that
takes New Testament ecclesiology to heart, this book is for you. Knight takes
us down ancient paths and shows how they lead to healthy church growth.
His advice may not be what you want, but it is certainly what you need as a
church-pastoring church planter. The path is hard, but it will produce a church
that can endure hardship; it may be laborious, but it is the surest way to plant.
It may be painful, but it will result in a healthy, strong church that presents
and protects the gospel. Read this book, preach the gospel, love God's people,
rest in faith, and watch the Lord of the church do his work."

Dieudonné Tamfu, Pastor, Bethlehem Baptist Church, Yaoundé,
Cameroon; Assistant Professor of Bible and Theology and
Executive Director of the Cameroon Extension Site, Bethlehem
College & Seminary

"Biblical faithfulness and faith in God are twin essentials for church planting.
Follow the Master's guidelines and trust the Master for the growth. This is the
thrust of this book, and I am glad to commend it to those who seek to plant
and grow biblically faithful churches for the glory of King Jesus."

Daniel L. Akin, President, Southeastern Baptist Theological
Seminary

"Nathan Knight has been a model for me of a pastor who serves with humility, faith, compassion, and zeal for the supremacy of Christ. In this inspiring book, Knight explains that a church plant can be healthy, despite being small, financially needy, or expanding slowly, even if it is growing more deeply than it spreads. Using Jesus as the reference point, Knight invites us to view church planters as shepherds and church plants as biblical churches. He contends that shepherds ought to display godly character, capability, conviction, confidence, and compassion. He encourages sending churches to care for and watch over church planters. The book presents wise strategic advice and important lessons learned by suffering for Christ."

Déholo Nali, Pastor, Connexion Rockland, Rockland, Ontario

"Church planters and leaders are drowning in too many opportunities, pressures, and ideas. Deep down we feel like we're failing even when it looks like we're 'successful.' In *Planting by Pastoring*, Nathan Knight thrusts hope into our hearts with the Bible's truth and goodness. He clarifies our roles, tools, and goals with simplicity and utility so that we rest in and move with Jesus in planting by pastoring. Find refreshment here for the good work Christ has for you."

P. J. Tibayan, Pastor, Bethany Baptist Church, Bellflower, California; blogger, SaintPJ.com

Planting by Pastoring

Planting by Pastoring

A Vision for Starting a Healthy Church

Nathan Knight

:: CROSSWAY®

WHEATON, ILLINOIS

Trade paperback ISBN: 978-1-4335-8811-2
ePub ISBN: 978-1-4335-8814-3
PDF ISBN: 978-1-4335-8812-9

Library of Congress Cataloging-in-Publication Data

Names: Knight, Nathan, 1975– author.
Title: Planting by pastoring : a vision for starting a healthy church / Nathan Knight.
Description: Wheaton, Illinois : Crossway, 2023. | Series: 9marks | Includes bibliographical references and index.
Identifiers: LCCN 2022054987 (print) | LCCN 2022054988 (ebook) | ISBN 9781433588112 (trade paperback) | ISBN 9781433588129 (pdf) | ISBN 9781433588143 (epub)
Subjects: LCSH: Church development, New. | Church growth.
Classification: LCC BV652.25 .K63 2023 (print) | LCC BV652.25 (ebook) | DDC 254/.5—dc23/eng/20230417
LC record available at https://lccn.loc.gov/2022054987
LC ebook record available at https://lccn.loc.gov/2022054988

Crossway is a publishing ministry of Good News Publishers.

VP		32	31	30	29	28	27	26	25	24	23
15	14	13	12	11	10	9	8	7	6	5	4	3	2	1

To Joey, Page, and my beloved wife.
Where would we be without Christ and one another?

Contents

Series Preface

THE 9MARKS SERIES of books is premised on two basic ideas. First, the local church is far more important to the Christian life than many Christians today perhaps realize.

Second, local churches grow in life and vitality as they organize their lives around God's Word. God speaks. Churches should listen and follow. It's that simple. When a church listens and follows, it begins to look like the One it is following. It reflects his love and holiness. It displays his glory. A church will look like him as it listens to him.

So our basic message to churches is, don't look to the best business practices or the latest styles; look to God. Start by listening to God's Word again.

Out of this overall project comes the 9Marks series of books. Some target pastors. Some target church members. Hopefully all will combine careful biblical examination, theological reflection, cultural consideration, corporate application, and even a bit of individual exhortation. The best Christian books are always both theological and practical.

It is our prayer that God will use this volume and the others to help prepare his bride, the church, with radiance and splendor for the day of his coming.

With hope,
Jonathan Leeman
Series Editor

Introduction

SIZE, SPEED, SUFFICIENCY, AND SPREAD.

These four *s*'s determine success and significance in church plant-ing. Grow, grow, grow as fast as you can! Be financially self-sufficient sooner rather than later! Spread your impact by multiplying services or campuses or churches! If church planting were a sports car, then the four *s*'s would be its whirring engine; you can't see it, but it's there under the hood, powering everything. It sounds powerful and impressive. It purrs and hums. Who wouldn't want to drive that thing?

But what if we popped the hood and discovered that this engine needed work? What if the engine sounded nice, but we knew this engine wasn't built to last? What if the engine merely looked good, but actually endangered passengers?

This is a pop-the-hood book. Its goal is to ask the questions of the previous paragraph, applying them to church planting. What if the four *s*'s aren't what your church plant needs to run on? What if we should look elsewhere for success and significance?

Oh, but size and speed and sufficiency and spread are so enticing! We all want them. I know I did when I first started out. I wanted more people to hear the gospel, and I wanted those people to come quickly so that we would "make it" without external financial support. And yeah, I wanted—and still want!—to spread the gospel into other communities through more church planting.

Every church planter should pursue the four *s*'s. But is pursuing them *the point* of church planting? Is achieving them the goal of church planting? Can a church planter be successful without size and speed and sufficiency and spread?

Yes, I think so. I hope to persuade you of that in this book. But first, let's talk a bit more about the four *s*'s. Are they really that prominent?

Size and Speed

Church planters love books. We love instructional manuals and manifestos and how-tos and everything in between. Popular church-planting literature places a great emphasis on the four *s*'s. Let's talk about the first two for a moment—size and speed.

Nelson Searcy comes right out and says it: "As you think about the launch date for your church, remember that your primary goal is to launch as publicly as possible, with as many people as possible."[1] Ron Sylvia agrees, and in doing so lumps Jesus in with him: "Launching large is congruent with the best of missionary theology and with the Methods of Jesus."[2]

And then there's Ed Stetzer—perhaps the most popular purveyor of church-planting wisdom.[3] In *Planting Missional Churches*, Stetzer

---

1 Nelson Searcy, *Launch: Starting a New Church from Scratch* (Grand Rapids, MI: Baker, 2017), 124.

2 Ron Sylvia, *Starting New Churches on Purpose: Strategies for the 21st Century* (Lake Forest, CA: Purpose Driven, 2006), 108.

3 "Books by Ed Stetzer," EdStetzer.com, accessed August 31, 2022, https://edstetzer.com /books/.

and Daniel Im say "reproduction is the goal—reproducing believers, ministries, groups, and churches."[4]

"Rapid mobilization" is often thought to be central to church-planting success since it spreads the gospel to more people more quickly. Stetzer and Warren Bird advocate this approach in their book *Viral Churches*: "Our hope is to inspire and help you develop a church multiplication movement—an exponential birth of new churches that engage lost people and that replicate themselves through even more new churches. A church multiplication movement is a rapid reproduction of churches planting churches."[5]

Steve Addison follows suit in *Movements That Change the World*. He lists "rapid mobilization" as one of the requirements for global change.[6] Dave Ferguson, president of America's largest church-planting conference, writes in his book *Exponential* that "Jesus has given his church the problem of rapid reproduction."[7]

Without question, common church-planting wisdom says size and speed are vital to success. However, when we consider Scripture, we find a narrative not of speed but of slowness, so that God might be glorified as his people put their trust in him.

Consider Abraham and Sarah, who were childless for nearly twenty-five years after God's promise. Or Israel, who endured slavery in Egypt for 420 years before their deliverance. Or the coming of Christ, which happened thousands of years after God's initial

---

4   Ed Stetzer and Daniel Im, *Planting Missional Churches: Your Guide to Starting Churches That Multiply* (Nashville, TN: B&H Academic, 2016), 121.

5   Ed Stetzer and Warren Bird, *Viral Churches: Helping Church Planters Become Movement Makers* (San Francisco, CA: Jossey-Bass, 2010), 5.

6   Steve Addison, *Movements That Change the World* (Downers Grove, IL: InterVarsity Press, 2011), 24.

7   Dave Ferguson and Jon Ferguson, *Exponential: How You and Your Friends Can Start a Missional Church Movement* (Grand Rapids, MI: Zondervan, 2010), 14.

promise in Genesis 3:15. Or consider Christians right now, who have been longing for Christ's return for more than two thousand years. As my old mentor used to say to me, "God is rarely early, but he's never late."

Self-Sufficiency

Now let's talk about the third *s*: self-sufficiency.

Think for a moment about how we refer to church plants that don't make it. "Failed," we often say. If, after a long enough time, there simply aren't enough people or money to go around, then the church planters have "failed" at their mission.

This sentiment dominates the landscape. Just consider these comments from a so-called "failed" church planter: "In the end, the church plant did not last. After thousands of dollars raised and about fifteen months of effort, it failed. I simply could not get enough traction when gathering. I was underfunded. I lacked experience. I was alone. I had heart, and I had zeal."[8]

Not enough money. Not enough people. Failure. When I read this, I wanted to reach through my screen and grab the author and tell him, "Oh, brother, you didn't fail!"

It is true that 1 Timothy 5:8 commands us to provide for our families; however, financial profitability has zero bearing upon the essence of what makes for successful church planting. I suspect a hard-working church planter who, over the course of many years, can't gain *any* traction with people apart from his family generally might need to move on to something else. I'm not arguing that church planters should never give up. It's the relationship of size and survivability as "essential" that is dangerous.

---

8   Gavin Pate, "Why I Am No Longer a Church Planter," The Gospel Coalition, June 17, 2014, https://www.thegospelcoalition.org.

Too many planters can subconsciously begin to believe that the essence of a church is its financial success (or lack of). Few might think this consciously, but I fear many think it subconsciously. Consequently, when a financial goal isn't met within five years, they can believe they've failed to plant a church. Or, perhaps they think they've failed as individuals. Maybe the planters do need to move on, but it's not because they lack the essence of what makes a church plant.

Think about impoverished areas in your community or in Bangkok, Thailand. Churches need to be planted there, and yet, we might assume they will never be financially viable. Yet, insofar as they are doing the basic elements of what makes a church a church, they can thrive more than the prosperity gospel "church" down the street that has throngs of people coming in and out of it each week along with huge financial windfalls. That church has failed; the biblically faithful church plant hasn't.

Kenneth Jones, a fellow pastor in Washington, DC, planted Redeemer City church eight years ago. To date, the church has not been able to fully support him financially. Not only does he continue on, but more importantly, the work of the church continues on. He said to me recently, "Our church is small, but we gather and preach the gospel every week, we participate in the ordinances together, members are cared for, and our neighbors are hearing about Christ. The size of our gathering or the size of our bank account hasn't stopped the work of our church."

Spread

So far we've seen that speed, size, and self-sufficiency often become the litmus test for a church plant's success. But there's one other factor—one that usually happens after self-sufficiency is reached—

that also looms large. I'm talking about spread. Generally speaking, church plants aren't successful until they've spread their influence through multiplication.

Continuing in their book *Viral Churches*, Stetzer and Bird say that for a church-planting movement of multiplication to occur, there need to be new markers of success: "The better option is to develop new benchmarks, such as a more organic mind-set that focuses on abundance verses size. . . . Perhaps we need to think more like farmers, hungering for the orchard that we're helping to plant to become wildly out of control."[9]

What are these "new benchmarks" for achieving a church-planting movement? In short, Stetzer and Bird encourage the planter to focus on an abundant amount of church plants, not simply larger gatherings. The more churches there are, the more we can keep up with population growth. If we can achieve this, then we will successfully achieve a church-planting movement. But the goal is exponential multiplication.

We see this in church-planting literature, but we also see it in church-planting events. Perhaps the largest conference on church planting, Exponential, produced a field guide that teaches planters how to become a "level five" multiplying church.[10] On their website, you can take the "multiplication challenge" and, in the process, unlock your church's potential by "launching more churches with greater success." You can even find a list of reproducing churches and, upon following their advice, build a legacy as an exponential church-planting church.[11]

---

9 Stetzer and Bird, *Viral Churches*, 202.
10 Todd Wilson, et al., *Becoming a Level Five Multiplying Church: Field Guide* (Exponential, 2015).
11 Reproducing Churches website, accessed September 1, 2022, https://reproducingchurches .org/.

Let's talk about books again. One popular church-planting website listed the top ten church-planting books of 2019. Four of the ten are explicitly related to multiplication or spread.[12] Some of the brightest lights in the Southern Baptist world consider multiplication necessary for a healthy church. J. D. Greear, the former president of the Southern Baptist Convention and the pastor of Summit Church, writes that the greatness of the church is not in its seating capacity but in its sending capacity.[13]

While I trust that Greear would in no way mean to pit multiplying against growing in depth, we need to make clear that multiplication doesn't come at the expense of depth. When we aim so much at reaching more people, it becomes easy to look past the ones that are already here. We become like so much of the church in America, a mile wide and an inch deep.

Imagine a book on parenting that urged you to have as many children as possible as quickly as possible because children are a blessing from the Lord. Now imagine the book never addresses how to meaningfully serve, love, and discipline those children. That would be a bad book; I hope you wouldn't read it and recommend it to others.

But what would *the result* be if people took that book's advice to heart? Large families that were unhealthy and poorly provided for. I fear the same might be said in certain corners of our church-planting conversations. We're inviting planters to join a movement that leaves its families malnourished and its children anonymous.

---

12 Daniel Yang, "Top 10 Church Planting Related Books from 2019," Send Institute, December 10, 2019, https://www.sendinstitute.org.

13 J. D. Greear, "Plumb Line #2: We Judge Our Success by Sending Capacity, Not Seating Capacity," J. D. Greear Ministries, October 5, 2016, https://jdgreear.com.

I can't tell you how many times I've had members, attenders, and nonbelievers over to my home, where they expressed a level of shock to have dinner with "the pastor." Time and again, these people tell me that their pastor was often an elusive figure "up there" on the stage—not someone in their lives, not someone who knew them and checked in on them. I've had to convince certain members to come and talk to me about problems they're facing or decisions they're weighing because they thought I was "too busy" for them. Too busy doing what? I thought this was what we do?

Our church also has had Christians show up for months without committing. When asked why, they tell us that it's because they've never been taught that committing to a church actually means something. Church has been like Verizon or Burger King; you tap into the service and leave when you're full. If you get tired of the church, then you move on to the next one, like switching to Sprint or Wendy's. After all, no pastor or church leader would even notice.

Perhaps saddest of all, we sometimes meet Christians who have followed Jesus for decades—men and women who have been part of several churches. When they learn that we spend half our elders' meetings giving brief updates on members and then praying for them individually, they can't believe it. They'd never been individually known, heard, and prayed for like that.

Are We Missing Something?

Size, speed, self-sufficiency, and spread aren't inherently bad goals. I trust that the authors quoted above are eager and godly and well-intentioned. They want to spread the gospel just like I do. They want to see churches planted just like I do.

Ultimately, however, our intentions matter less than our ideas. Ideas have consequences. Focusing on four good things at the exclusion of other good things has ramifications. So let's back off the gas pedal for a moment and ask some questions that may lead to some different practices—or at least some different emphases.

What is a church?
How would you know when you planted or started one?
What does a church do?
What are the ordinances? What do they have to do with a church?
What is a pastor? What does he have to do with a church?

In sum: Where's *the church* in all these church-planting resources?

It seems to me that the emphasis on size, speed, sufficiency, and spread leaves individual people behind, as well as the family life that Jesus intends for those individual people. It seems to prioritize their being "reached" over their being "formed." I don't know about you, but most people I know struggle to follow Jesus. They wrestle against sin in their marriages and in their singleness, on the job and in the home. They face suffering. They wonder where God is.

When we aim to reach people and reproduce them quickly, it becomes difficult to actually minister to them as Jesus did. It becomes difficult to get up close and personal, as a family does. How do you slow down to love people who struggle to follow Jesus when size and speed and spread are so important? Planting by pastoring is glorious and grace-filled work. But it's inefficient work.

I want to ask one more question: Where's the worship? We're told that the goal of church planting is to reach the lost. But is that the proper goal? It's most certainly critical to the work of church planting, but surely evangelism isn't the finish line.

I'm reminded of a John Piper quote that's pretty famous, at least in the Christian world. "Missions is not the ultimate goal of the church. Worship is. Missions exists because worship doesn't."[14] This isn't some "Jesus juke." Piper's right. Worship *is* the heart of our life together as a church. The goal isn't size or speed, sufficiency or spread. The goal is to know and enjoy Christ Jesus the Lamb of God who takes away the sin of the world (John 1:29; 17:3)—but to do all of that *together*. The goal is to worship now in light of how we will worship in heaven (Rev. 5:8–10).

What Is Success?

I've spent enough time telling you what church-planting success is *not*. It's not what you read in most church-planting books, and it's not what you'll find at most church-planting conferences. So what does success in church planting look like?

It looks like biblically defined churches led by biblically qualified pastors who lead the church to worship and enjoy the risen Savior together as a family. We want to plant oak trees not dandelions. We want to know names, not numbers—stories, not statistics. We want to look out every week and see a family, not just friendly but anonymous faces. And at the center of the family is Jesus Christ.

Michael Reeves writes in his book *Rejoicing in Christ*:

We naturally gravitate, it seems toward *anything* but Jesus—and Christians almost as much as anyone—whether it's the "Christian worldview," "grace," "the Bible" or "the gospel," as if they were things *in themselves* that could save us. Even the "the cross" can get abstracted from Jesus, as if the wood had some power of its own. Other things, wonderful things, vital concepts, beautiful discoveries so easily edge *Jesus* aside. Precious theological concepts

---

14 John Piper, *Let the Nations Be Glad!*, 3rd ed. (Grand Rapids, MI: Baker Academic, 2010), 15.

meant to describe *him* and *his* work get treated as things in their own right. He becomes just another brick in the wall. But the center, the cornerstone, the jewel in the crown of Christianity is not an idea, a system or a thing; it is not even "the gospel" as such. It is Jesus Christ.[15]

We could easily add "church planting" to this list of things that can get abstracted from Jesus. Eternal life isn't merely establishing witnesses and multiplying them across the city as quickly as possible. Eternal life, Jesus says, is knowing him and the Father who sent him. We plant churches to pastor individual people so that they will treasure Christ individually and we will treasure Christ corporately. That's the goal, the point, the true north of church planting.

If you want to be a church planter but you haven't spent much time ministering to people yet, you're soon going to find out that they are fickle. Ask the average planter what life was like in the weeks, months, and years *after* their large "launch" service. Most will tell you it was and remains a mess.

So church planter, you're going to need more than a commitment to your personal "calling" in order to plant a church. You're going to need more than "proven strategies" that you found on a popular website. You're going to need steel in order to stand, and God has provided that steel by outlining what a church is and does in his word.

I hope to convince you of something simple and precious over the course of this book. I hope to convince you that if you want your life to count, then seek to know the names and faces and stories

---

15 Michael Reeves, *Rejoicing in Christ* (Downers Grove, IL: IVP Academic, 2015), 10.

and wins and losses of real people. Seek to gather these people under the protection of a Christ-enjoying, biblically defined church. And seek to stay there for the long haul and plant more churches.

Planting by Pastoring: What Lies Ahead

We'll begin by noting how the thrust of Scripture presses us toward Jesus, who came to plant his church as a pastor not an entrepreneur. After this, we'll consider what it looks like to plant as pastors ourselves. This will lead us into biblical definitions for who is qualified to do this important work, followed by some clarity as to what this thing we are trying to start actually is and does. We'll then consider the culture of the church and the goal of the church as Christ, not ourselves or consumerism.

With the car and its engine built, we'll put some paint on the car by thinking about being planted by a church and not a parachurch organization. Then we'll consider what it looks like to plant as a team not an individual. This will be followed by some analysis about where to plant and expectations once we get on the ground. We'll then consider who and how we might go after folks in evangelism and discipleship. Our final chapter will examine what healthy multiplication looks like.

By the end of this book, we should know what constitutes success and significance in the important work of church planting. If you're looking for market-friendly strategies, then you won't like what you're about to read. But if you've tried the best of those and found them wanting, then I think you'll find some help in what's ahead.

PART 1

CHURCH-PLANTING
RESIDENCY

1

Jesus as Shepherd

The Prince of Planters

IN 2009, pastor Kevin DeYoung began a sermon with Jesus's provocative question to Peter in Matthew 16:15: "Who do you say that I am?" DeYoung documents how different circles in America answer that question today:

There's Republican Jesus who is against tax increases and activist judges, and for family values and owning firearms.

There's Democrat Jesus who is against Wall Street and Walmart, for reducing our carbon footprint and spending other people's money.

There's Therapist Jesus who helps us cope with life's problems, heals our past, tells us how valuable we are and not to be so hard on ourselves.

There's Starbucks Jesus who drinks fair trade coffee, loves spiritual conversations, drives a hybrid, and goes to film festivals. . . .

There's Touchdown Jesus who helps athletes run faster and jump higher than non-Christians and determines the outcomes of Super Bowls.[1]

We're all more guilty than we'd like to admit that we sometimes worship a Jesus who fits in the comfortable confines of our personal interests. This is true even for pastors. DeYoung could have added "church-planting Jesus" to his list—the Jesus who esteems movements and multiplication over everything else.

The real Jesus, however, confronts our most basic assumptions about church planting. What if his vision for the church were less like McDonald's, which serves billions and billions across the world, and more like your family kitchen, which serves your family members and dearest friends? What if Jesus treasured knowing his sheep's names? What if he wanted to walk alongside them through good days and hard days, helping them obey all that he commanded?

Failed Pastors

But before we get to how Jesus approached his pastoral ministry, we need to go further back in time. We need to understand that Jesus came to fix a big problem.

Imagine yourself living in the days of Ezekiel, long before the coming of Christ. There you are, among the other exiles of Judah in the land of Babylon. It's a hot afternoon in your new home. Life is still strange in this foreign place, but you're getting used to it. You bend down at the riverside and cup some water to wash your face. As you do, you see some leaders of the tribe of Judah. You can't help but scoff. These so-called "leaders" do nothing but lay

1   Kevin DeYoung, "Who Do You Say That I Am?," The Gospel Coalition, November 20, 2014, https://www.thegospelcoalition.org.

heavy burdens on you and your family. They like to appeal to the Law, yet their interest in you is faint. Just last week your daughter was injured in a serious fall. One of these so-called shepherds of Israel entered your home and didn't even look at your daughter. He coldly demanded a tithe and stormed out.

These leaders dress nicely as you struggle to clothe your family. They feast while you scrounge for a few unleavened cakes of bread. But they're happy to tell you all that God demands of you while you scrape to make a life as an exile.

With the water still rolling down your face, you hear a familiar voice—Ezekiel's. This prophet's words are hard to take sometimes, but you know he speaks the truth. Ezekiel begins to preach:

> Thus says the Lord GOD: Ah, shepherds of Israel who have been feeding yourselves! Should not shepherds feed the sheep? You eat the fat, you clothe yourselves with the wool, you slaughter the fat ones, but you do not feed the sheep. The weak you have not strengthened, the sick you have not healed, the injured you have not bound up, the strayed you have not brought back, the lost you have not sought, and with force and harshness you have ruled them. (Ezek. 34:2–4)

You head back to your tent with a smile as you say to yourself: "Go get 'em, Ezekiel. I can't help but wonder what things would be like if we actually had *good* shepherds. We certainly wouldn't be here, that's for sure."

Jesus, the Shepherd

Later, Ezekiel explains why this scattering—this exile—happened. "Because there was no shepherd, and [the people] became food for all the wild beasts" (Ezek. 34:5). Incensed by these selfish "shepherds," the Lord promised to come down and shepherd his people himself:

> I myself will be the shepherd of my sheep, and I myself will make them lie down, declares the Lord GOD. . . . I will set up over them one shepherd, my servant David, and he shall feed them: he shall feed them and be their shepherd. And I, the LORD, will be their God, and my servant David shall be prince among them. (Ezek. 34:15, 23–24)

I've often wondered how the Israelites heard this promise. It had to have been somewhat confusing for them. David was long dead, so how would he come back? Who is Ezekiel talking about here? I bet they had a lot of questions—at least until Jesus showed up.

Jesus Christ is the fulfillment of this promise. He is the servant, *the* shepherd. He shows up and says, "I am the good shepherd. The good shepherd lays his life down for the sheep . . . I am the good shepherd. I know my own and my own know me" (John 10:11, 14). Everyone knew what he was talking about. Over and over again, Jesus identified himself as a shepherd, a pastor. He saw himself that way, and his closest followers saw him that way. Mark tells us in his Gospel that when Jesus looked upon the crowds, he was filled with compassion because they were like "sheep without a shepherd" (Mark 6:34). So he went and taught them. Isaiah describes him the same way: "He will tend his flock like a shepherd; he will gather the lambs in his arms; he will carry them in his bosom, and gently lead those that are with young" (Isa. 40:11).

The Father sent his Son as a shepherd because that's what his people need. It's what they've always needed so that they wouldn't scatter or go astray.

Jesus, the Pastor-Planter

We know Jesus is a shepherd because he calls himself one. But even if he'd never used the title, we would still see his shepherd's heart by observing his ministry—how he prayed, how he loved and taught, how he shared authority, and ultimately how he sacrificed himself.

Jesus prayed. I used to think a day of prayer and solitude was time *away* from the mission. Jesus saw it the other way around. As he went about planting his church and the crowds pressed in, Jesus's instinct was to pull away frequently in order to pray (Mark 1:35; Luke 5:16; 6:12). As he faced the agony of the cross, he steeled himself with an intense session of prayer (Luke 22:39–46). Jesus was planting as a pastor, and pastors pray.

Jesus loved and taught. While lounging at a dinner party with the town elites, Jesus didn't see the sinful woman who interrupted the meeting as a distraction, but as an opportunity to love and teach. A parable of grace and forgiveness came effortlessly from his lips as the woman wept and the town elites mocked (Luke 7:36–50). He was willing to lose face with the movers and shakers in order to shepherd one single, burdened woman. Jesus was planting as a pastor, and pastors love and teach.

Jesus shared authority. When it came time for Jesus to call his closest followers, he didn't select the gifted and the powerful, but instead chose twelve fumbling men—a few nondescript fishermen, a despised tax collector, and so on. After a period of discipleship, he then "gave them authority" and sent them out in pairs so that they would "proclaim that people should repent" (Mark 6:7, 12).

Notice two things in this passage. First, Jesus took advantage of his popularity to give authority away. Second, he gave authority away in order to see people repent and believe. Jesus was planting as a pastor, and pastors share authority in order that more and more people might proclaim the gospel and be won to that gospel through faith and repentance.

Jesus sacrificed himself. Perhaps most amazing of all, Jesus "remained silent" (Matt. 26:63) as he stood before the unjust Sanhedrin, hearing false charge after false charge leveled against him. It's tempting to wonder why. After all, Jesus was heaven's darling! He threw demons into pigs! We want him to speak up for himself, to rebuke these fools and make the truth known.

Eventually he does speak up, and in doing so he explains his silence. Blood dripping from his brow, he says, "For this purpose I was born and for this purpose I have come into the world—to bear witness to the truth. Everyone who is of the truth listens to my voice" (John 18:37). Jesus remained silent so that he might sacrifice his life in order to bring his sheep into the way, the truth, and the life. Jesus was planting as a pastor, and pastors sacrifice for the good of their people in order to bear witness to the truth.

Sturdy Church

Remember the children's story *The Three Little Pigs*? The first pig built his house out of straw. The second pig built his house out of sticks. The third built his house out of bricks. You know how this goes. Because the first two houses were hastily built, the wolf easily blew them down. But the house made of bricks stood up to the enemy. Building with bricks took the third pig longer, he endured scorn from others, and he probably missed out on some fun on account of his difficult task. Nevertheless, because he was careful, slow, patient, and wise, he didn't lose his house.

The church is like that third pig's house. Jesus came to "build [his] church" so that the "gates of hell [would] not prevail against it" (Matt. 16:18). Writing to one of his church plants, Paul says, "No one can lay a foundation other than that which is laid, which is Jesus Christ. Now if anyone builds on the foundation with gold, silver, precious stones, wood, hay, straw—each one's work will become manifest, for the Day will disclose it, because it will be revealed by fire, and the fire will test what sort of work each one has done" (1 Cor. 3:11–13).

Jesus didn't hastily build the church. He was deliberate and careful. He prioritized relationships over speed. Jesus was a pastor. He planted his church as a pastor. He knew his sheep and his sheep knew him. He drew near to them. He cared for them. He led them, gently. He listened and ministered to individuals. Names, not numbers, concerned him. He looked people in the eye, he touched their wounds, he wept with them, he entered their homes, he shared meals, he washed their feet, he taught them the truth, and he prayed for them. His pastoral work laid a foundation for the church that survives the "big bad wolf."

Churches built on Jesus and his gospel will survive on the last day. If you're a church planter or pastor, it's worth asking the question, What lies at the foundation of this thing I've spent such a long time building?

The Freedom of Planting the Hard Way

Tyrone, Edna, Sarah, Matt, and Laurie. These five people—and countless more—have made me slow down in ministry. You'll meet each of them as we discuss planting by pastoring. They've made me love hard. You won't find commendations of slowness in many planting resources, but I encourage you to add it to your church-planting strategy. It's absolutely vital.

Let the size and significance of your ministry take care of themselves. Slow down and press the gospel into people's lives, just like Jesus did. He doesn't want us to be shepherds that feed themselves or shepherds that long for crowds or movements more than they long for people. Jesus wants us to be shepherds who feed others God's word by sharing the eternal worth of Christ Jesus, our Lord, our Savior, our King, and our treasure.

Pastors, not entrepreneurs. Shepherds, not salesmen. That's what my city needs. That's what your town needs. So let's dive in and consider what it would look like to plant a church by pastoring people into the excellencies of our great shepherd.

2

Pastors, Not Entrepreneurs

The Posture of the Planter

ON A CRISP FALL EVENING IN 2009, my coplanter, Joey Craft, and I decided it was time to start gathering some people for our church plant. We had been in Washington, DC, only a few months. We didn't know anyone when we landed, so we spent an enormous amount of energy getting to know and serve our community.

We asked a church in Georgia to buy us a box of Tim Keller's *Prodigal God*. We passed the books out to folks we had built relationships with. We asked them to join us in my apartment for a book discussion. The day came, and no one showed.

"What are we going to do now?" I wondered.

Finally, someone knocked on the door. A couple of college kids we'd met from George Washington University actually showed up! Not long after, a few coworkers from the Starbucks I worked at part-time also came. Before long, we had about eight randomly collected individuals. What's more, they came back the next week. Then others joined, and they started bringing friends with them.

I sometimes look back at those times and wonder why these people came. I know the ultimate answer is that the Spirit of God was drawing them to himself. And yet, besides that, I remember that these people genuinely believed we wanted something *for* them, not something *from* them. From the very beginning, they believed we were aiming to be pastors not entrepreneurs. They knew we cared about their souls.

"Men Whom the Multitudes Would Follow"

As we've seen, Jesus understood himself to be a pastor. He didn't heal and preach to gather nameless crowds. In fact, he sometimes scattered crowds that gathered to use him rather than love him (John 6:66). As Robert Coleman says in his book *The Master Plan of Evangelism*:

> [Jesus's] concern was not with programs to reach the multitudes, but with men whom the multitudes would follow. Remarkable as it may seem, Jesus started to gather these men before he ever organized an evangelistic campaign or even preached a sermon in public. Men were to be his method of winning the world to God.[1]

Our church didn't have the most auspicious beginnings. Before arriving in DC, I had only preached a handful of times. We weren't sent by a large church. We weren't from the area. At the beginning, we didn't even have any music. And when we finally did start singing, it would occasionally feature me sitting down playing Chris Tomlin songs, followed by my standing up to preach (weird, I know). We had a website, but we didn't put our church

1   Robert Emerson Coleman and Billy Graham, *The Master Plan of Evangelism* (Grand Rapids, MI: Revell, 2008), 21.

address on there because it also happened to be the same place my wife and one-year-old son slept. Visitors had to email us to find out where we met. This is probably not a script worth following, but the Lord used it.

We never blitzed the neighborhood with mailers. We didn't utilize our website like we probably could have. We didn't hold a "preview" or launch service. In fact, the closest thing we had to a formal "launch" was a service where eighteen of us covenanted together as church members in front of about fifteen others in a one-time rental of a Baptist church building that didn't even have a working baptistry (more on that later).

So, what *did* we do? We had folks over for dinner. We went on walks. We preached. We discipled people at Starbucks. In everything we did, we tried to communicate authentic interest in real people. We wedded biblical truth to a deep love for Jesus—that's about it.

Here's what's wonderful about all this: it didn't cost much. So these same "strategies" are available to you. People came for our Bible studies, our discipling groups, and our church services not because we had such magnetic personalities. They came because they could tell we wanted to care for them as their shepherds, to guide them in the ancient paths of our glorious Savior. They felt listened to and loved.

What about Being Entrepreneurial?

Church-planting resources regularly encourage church planters to see themselves as entrepreneurs. Planters are told they *need* imagination, creativity, and a keen sense of cultural exegesis in order to start a church in our modern Western world. The old way of "doing church" doesn't work. We need folks who, like business leaders, "leverage the networking and value the creation they've seen businesses master to form communities of Christ followers among unchurched people."[2]

Broadly speaking, I'm happy to encourage planters to be entrepreneurial. Consider Paul's example in Romans 15:20: "I make it my ambition to preach the gospel, not where Christ has already been named, lest I build on someone else's foundation." Paul is at least somewhat entrepreneurial. He dreams about starting new churches in desolate places. Or think of how he used a cultural reference point—the "unknown God"—in the Areopagus in Acts 17 to point to Jesus.

But Paul's chief concern wasn't developing his entrepreneurial ingenuity. He simply wanted to make sure these churches were cared for by faithful shepherds. That's why he told his church-planting resident Titus to "appoint elders in every town" (Titus 1:5). He then lists the qualifications of pastors in the following verses—qualifications that focus on character not giftedness. He does the same for Timothy (1 Tim. 3:1–7).

In fact, we see a glimpse of Paul's pastoral heart as he leaves his Ephesian church plant in tears, reminding the Ephesian pastors that he went "house to house" and taught them the "whole counsel of God" (Acts 20:17–38). He admonishes them to carry out the same type of ministry he carried out among them, paying "careful attention to yourselves and to all the flock, in which the Holy Spirit has made you overseers to care for the church of God, which he obtained with his own blood" (Acts 20:28).

Paul, like Jesus, trained future leaders to love their flocks and to meet the qualifications of a pastor. His chief interest, like Jesus, was pastoral not numerical. He never abandoned a fledgling flock because

2   Jay Moon, *A Missional Approach to the Marketplace* (Exponential, 2019), 10.

they required too much. Paul knew firsthand that the Christian life was warfare (Eph. 6:10–20) and that far too many wouldn't endure but would succumb to the lures of this world (2 Tim. 4:10). He also knew that the church ought to be the pillar and buttress of the truth (1 Tim. 3:15), the manifold wisdom and the glory of God (Eph. 3:10, 21). Therefore, he planted churches as often and as strategically as he could, but only insofar as they were led by gospel-loving pastors.

Pastors vs. Entrepreneurs

What exactly is the difference between a pastorally inclined planter versus an entrepreneurially inclined planter?

One quick way to discover where you land is asking how you define success in church planting. As we mentioned, entrepreneur-planters will often emphasize the four *s*'s: size, speed, self-sustainability, and spread. These equal success.

Pastor-planters, however, will slow down. They might sacrifice speed and size to make sure people clearly understand both the gospel and the church. Pastor-planters aim at something less flashy: simply starting a biblically defined church. They are, after all, *church* planters. We'll talk about this more in chapter 4, but for now, a church can be defined as:

> A covenanted group of Christians that gathers regularly together to hear the preaching of the gospel and affirm one another's membership in the gospel and in Christ's body through baptism and the Lord's Supper while protecting the gospel and that body through church discipline.

This goal—planting a church that meets the above criteria—may take some time. But it doesn't hinder the spread of the gospel. In fact, I'd argue this slow-going strategy actually *promotes* the gospel. Consider the apostles—whom Luke calls "uneducated, common men" (Acts 4:13). They simply preached the gospel boldly (Acts 4:1–4, 29, 33), and then gathered those who responded as a people of "one heart and soul" (Acts 4:32). The simple activity of "common men" preaching and loving those who responded eventually led the leaders of Jerusalem to throw them in prison (Acts 4:1–6). If you want to promote the gospel, then commit yourself to faithful preaching, fervent prayer, and radical love for one another. That's how "all people will know that you are my disciples" (John 13:35).

Further still, this definition of success is robustly accessible to different types of leaders, and it doesn't need to sacrifice the good desire to spread the gospel far and wide.

This highlights another difference between the two types of planters. Entrepreneurially inclined planters typically emphasize strategy as much as they emphasize the patterns of Scripture. In his book *Launch*, Nelson Searcy tells the history of McDonald's and then concludes with this: "The principles of strategy development and application are just as *essential* to your success. Without a specific, well thought out strategic plan it is *impossible* to launch a successful restaurant, high school, library, zoo in Kalamazoo, or church."[3] Business-savvy strategy is thought to be the secret ingredient of the successful church. Thus the emphasis on the word *entrepreneur*.

I don't want to understate the truth that church planters need a plan. They need to know what they're aiming at and how they hope to get there. But church planters also need to remember that it's not ultimately their strategies that bring about success. After all,

---

3 Nelson Searcy, *Launch: Starting a New Church from Scratch* (Grand Rapids, MI: Baker, 2017), 53. Emphasis added.

church plants are made up of people, and people are won by God's gospel—not by man's well-thought-out strategies. Furthermore, people are often won in surprising, unpredictable ways. Strategies help, but they're not foolproof. So pastor-planters strategize, but their ultimate hope is in bold and faithful gospel proclamation.

Related to their emphasis on strategy, entrepreneurial church planters tend to highlight the value of contextualization. In his book *Center Church*, Tim Keller writes, "Skill in contextualization is one of the keys to ministry today."[4] What does that word *contextualization* mean? It simply means the planter needs to know how to communicate the gospel to his immediate culture without compromising its message.

Some level of contextualization is unavoidable. Because I've planted in DC, I speak in English, not Portuguese. I wear jeans, not a kilt. And yes, I've tried to know the difference between a Democrat and a Republican. Of course, the pastorally minded planter is going to learn these things, too—not by cultivating some abstract "skill" but by simply learning to love those he lives among. In that sense, it's not our efforts at contextualization that enable our love for others; it's our love for others that serves our efforts at contextualization. Love comes first.

Pastor vs. Planter

Planters are pastors.

I used to recoil at that sentence. In my mind, pastors were characterized by slow work and halting growth. Sure, they worked to see the gospel spread, but they also had to deal with stuff like purging membership rolls, fixing HVAC systems, counseling troubled

4 Timothy Keller, *Center Church: Doing Balanced, Gospel-Centered Ministry in Your City* (Grand Rapids, MI: Zondervan, 2012), 90.

marriages, and confronting ungodly families that had outsized influence in their church.

Early on during seminary, I attended a conference and heard two men talk about the history of their particular local church. They talked about banal things like the drama that bubbled over after the pastor removed the American flag from the auditorium and the slow, inefficient work of tweaking the church's constitution and installing qualified elders. It all seemed both useful and extremely unspectacular. I couldn't help but think, *If this is most of a pastor's work, then I don't want to do that.*

I saw church planters as superheroes. They were the smart ones because they got to skip all that boring, inefficient, unspectacular stuff and jump straight into the more meaningful work of spreading the gospel and establishing a witness for Christ as quickly as possible.

I would tell people I chose planting because it "fits my personality." And isn't that what we all do? We look at a guy and say, "He'd make a good pastor . . . but I don't think he'd be an effective planter." Or vice versa. We've created a stereotype for "planters" that's related to but distinct from being a pastor.

But the Bible never holds out a stereotype for church planters. "Planter" isn't an office in the Bible. Instead, pastors and planters are after the same ends and should employ the same means of gospel ministry to get there. A pastor should be as ambitious as planters often are, and planters should care for the flock as pastors do. The best pastors are like planters, and the best planters are like pastors. Jesus is our model. He cared for those among him, yet desired spiritual good for those beyond that circle. He saw no dichotomy, and neither should we. The same could be said for Peter, Paul, and John—all of whom were committed evangelists and careful pastors.

Church planter isn't an additional office above or beyond or different from that of pastor-elder. Feel free to use the term (I do), and feel free to push certain brothers toward the task of planting, given their personality. But more than anything else—more than any calling to build something new—make sure you're aspiring to the old yet biblical model of who pastors are and what pastors do.

Sara

Not long after those initial Bible studies in my apartment, a woman named Sara visited our church. Sara was from Switzerland and had a PhD in biology from Oxford. She knew Christ, but she didn't know anything about belonging to a church. In fact, she told us in no uncertain terms on more than one occasion that she was not going to join our church because she didn't believe the Bible required church membership. We listened and kept loving. Sara kept coming and listening, too.

Sara's transition to the States proved difficult. As a result, some sisters in our church befriended her, providing encouragement and support. As Sara continued to attend, she formed a relationship with Joey and me. She shared meals with Joey's family. During these meals, Joey and his wife listened to her and prayed with her. On a number of occasions, Sara made Bible studies awkward with difficult comments, but we tried to respond gently, lovingly, and biblically.

Eventually, Sara began attending our church membership class. Even after the class, it took some time for her to get on board with the idea of joining a church. Nevertheless, she eventually committed herself to our fellowship. She's since moved back to Switzerland to join a church and make disciples there. Before she left, she told us that joining our church was one of the best decisions of her life.

She didn't say that merely because she'd become convinced church membership was in the Bible. She said that because brothers and sisters had walked with her, prayed with her, and answered her questions—not with human opinions, but with her precious Savior's words. She became convinced we loved her and were for her.

This is the glorious work Jesus wants for us in our churches. The Lord Jesus wants us to graciously shape real people into his image together as faith families. Brothers, pray that the Lord would grant you a holy ambition to start new churches! But even more, pray that the Lord would give you an ambition to form and pastor real people where Christ is not yet named so that they might know and enjoy him along with their brothers and sisters in Christ.

3

Qualified, Not Charismatic

The Character of the Planter

"YEAH, ONE MORE THING BEFORE WE GO," said one man in our community group.

We'd known each other for only a few months, but it was a committed crew. Our custom was—and still is—to break up into guys and gals after a brief word and some prayer so that we could have midweek accountability. Everything was new. Especially my preaching.

"I thought your sermon was boring," he said. The awkwardness in the room was palpable. Everyone's eyes were on me. How would I respond?

Here's what this brother didn't know before his not-so-helpful comment: I kind of agreed with him.

I was having a hard time with my preaching. Before planting a church, I'd never preached consecutive weeks. In fact, I hadn't preached more than five or six times in my life! So I struggled with the new normal. In addition to meeting new people and evangelizing the lost, I couldn't figure out how to put a sermon together—not to mention how to love my wife and my one-year-old son.

He didn't know all that—and the comment still crushed my ego. So I responded with a question: "Do you believe it is my job as a pastor to entertain you?"

The conversation that followed centered on the preacher's need to not be boring, yet still faithful. As Martin Lloyd-Jones said, "The preacher must never be dull, and he must never be boring. . . . How can a man be dull when he is handling such themes?"[1]

Qualified before Charismatic

On one level, that early church member was tapping into something I think all of us feel at the front end of planting a church: the need to be a better performer. This brother wanted me to be more alluring, more charismatic, more humorous. He wanted me to hold his attention such that I would keep him coming back every week.

This is certainly understandable. Most of us enjoy listening to faithful brothers like Matt Chandler, John Piper, David Platt, or Kevin DeYoung. And for good reason. These brothers *are* charismatic. They're funny, radiantly passionate, wicked smart, handsome, and/or comfortable in their own skin. I am none of these things. But the instinct to be those things in order to grow a church is strong, isn't it?

But even as we feel this understandable pull, we need to more properly assess and orient ourselves. We need to understand what's ultimately more stable and more alluring. As it's been said, "What you win them with is what you win them to."

---

1 D. Martyn Lloyd-Jones, *Preaching and Preachers* (London: Hodder, 2013), 100–101.

Charisma is helpful, important even. But I want to focus on other attributes that are even more important for the pastor: character, capability, conviction, and compassion.

Character

When Paul was writing to the church plant in Crete, he told Titus to "appoint elders in every town" so that he might "put what remained into order" (Titus 1:5). In case Titus might be unsure what elders should be like, Paul continued:

> . . . if anyone is above reproach, the husband of one wife, and his children are believers and not open to the charge of debauchery or insubordination. For an overseer, as God's steward, must be above reproach. He must not be arrogant or quick-tempered or a drunkard or violent or greedy for gain, but hospitable, a lover of good, self-controlled, upright, holy, and disciplined. (Titus 1:6–8)

He then explains to Titus why character is so important:

> For there are many who are insubordinate, empty talkers and deceivers, especially those of the circumcision party. They must be silenced, since they are upsetting whole families by teaching for shameful gain what they ought not to teach. One of the Cretans, a prophet of their own, said "Cretans are always liars, evil beasts, lazy gluttons." This testimony is true. (Titus 1:10–13)

Paul knows that if the church of Jesus Christ is going to testify to the holiness of God, it needs to be led by godly pastors. In other words, as Titus put what remained into order, he needed the character of the pastors to shine brightly against the dark night of the Crete skies. So it is with us.

Capability

For pastors, character is necessary but insufficient. They must also be "able to teach" (1 Tim. 3:2). Elsewhere, Paul says pastors need to "be able to give instruction in sound doctrine" (Titus 1:9).

The emphasis here is on clarity and biblical soundness. Is the pastor faithfully distinguishing between what is true and not true? A pastor's teaching doesn't need to be flashy, but it does need to be faithful and clear.

Conviction

Jesus was and is the truth (John 14:6). The church is the pillar and buttress of truth (1 Tim. 3:15). Therefore, every pastor-planter must have clear convictions about the truth. Paul says that "he *must* hold firm to the trustworthy word as taught" (Titus 1:9). What's true for deacons is surely true for pastor-planters: they must "hold the mystery of the faith with a clear conscience" (1 Tim. 3:9).

In our contemporary times, people often say things like, "What's true for you is true for you, and what's true for me is true for me." But that's not the Bible's attitude. What was true for Titus in Crete is true for pastors today. Pastors need to be men of conviction such that they "rebuke [the unbelieving] sharply, that they may be sound in the faith, not devoting themselves to Jewish myths and the commands of people who turn away from the truth" (Titus 1:13–14).

A brother must have orthodox convictions on Christianity's most vital doctrines: God, sin, Christ's work of salvation, and Scripture. Yet he also needs to have a strong understanding and convictions around those matters that protect the gospel and these first-tier doctrines, such as the church. People's consciences are being dulled, so the church needs leaders who will unashamedly teach and defend sound doctrine with joy and love.

Confidence

I can't help but wonder if we are so drawn to charismatic preachers because of their obvious confidence. Perhaps what we call "charisma" is actually just confidence.

I remember the first dozen or so times I watched John Piper preach. He certainly helped me see things in Scripture that I hadn't seen before. But in hindsight, I think I was more drawn to the serious confidence he took in the pulpit. This stuff was *real* and it was *important* and he exuded a kind of confidence I was drawn to. He wasn't posing questions without answering them. He wasn't doing hermeneutical gymnastics to avoid offending people. He was confident about the person, work, and worth of Christ.

According to Iain Murray, a Christian invited a lost man to an evangelistic meeting where Martyn Lloyd-Jones was preaching.[2] Lloyd-Jones thundered away with his usual authority, and the lost man didn't like it. The preacher was "arrogant," he said.

The man who had brought him disagreed. "Oh no," he said. "His confidence is not in himself, but in the word he preaches!"

That's it! Pastor-planters must radiate confidence in the historic truths of God's word.

Compassion

Finally, a pastor-planter must have a heart of compassion. Consider the tenderness of Jesus as he spoke to Martha (Luke 10:38–42). Or

2 "D. Martyn Lloyd-Jones: Pastor-Evangelist," panel discussion, Together for the Gospel, November 6, 2019, https://t4g.org/.

consider how easily Jesus spoke to children (Mark 10:13–16). Or how mercifully he approached the sinful woman in Luke 7:36–50. Peter says that pastor-planters must lead in a way that is "not domineering"; instead, they are "examples to the flock" (1 Pet. 5:3).

To be compassionate means to suffer together. It's not enough to have conviction; pastor-planters also need to model the love of Christ by having conviction *and* compassion. If you only have conviction, you'll be tempted to steamroll people. But if you only have compassion, you'll suffer with others, but not toward the truth. Pastor-planters will feel the pain in their people's and their community's lives. They will weep with those who weep and rejoice with those who rejoice (Rom. 12:15). And they will do so in the truth and with the truth. In doing so, they will build trust and bring the balm of the gospel to bear. Compassionate pastor-planters like this will reflect the heart of Christ in the pulpit and in living rooms.

We once had a member of our church who had a troubled up-bringing. His marriage was in trouble, and he was responding in many wrong ways. After listening to both spouses, I would insist that he should be more attentive to his wife's pains than he was to his own rights. I appealed to the truth, quoting Philippians 2:3–4 and Ephesians 5:25.

But I lacked compassion. I rarely expressed any sorrow over the ways his wife hurt him and made him feel unloved. I didn't suffer *with* him, and so my truthful counsel was difficult to hear. Later, however, I was able to grieve with him and even weep with him over the wrongs he had endured. He then was able to hear my counsel to love his wife as Christ loved the church.

We might have all the right answers. We might have character, capability, confidence, and conviction. But if we lack compassion, we are little more than clanging cymbals. Compassion wedded to the truth will lead to love, and love never fails (1 Cor. 13:8).

Emphasis Matters

I assume no faithful follower of Jesus will disagree with anything I've said. So why say it? My burden comes down to a matter of emphasis. What I'm trying to do in this book is to emphasize various essentials that are often assumed or taken for granted.

When these basic traits aren't the yogurt in the smoothie, when they're not the oil and gas in the car of church planting, then we'll emphasize other things and ultimately misconstrue what it means to be a pastor. If we say little about character, capability, confidence, and compassion, and a lot about the need for a planter to have a particular "calling" or a history of "starting something from nothing," then we've unintentionally begun to emphasize the nonessentials. We're talking about chia seeds and whey protein when we should be talking about yogurt and strawberries.

This misplaced emphasis creates a misplaced people. Consider for a moment what happens after a charismatic pastor falls from grace—maybe he strays morally, maybe he strays theologically. I've counseled church members through a number of those situations. In every case, I've wondered what would have happened had the pastor's sending church focused more on his character at the front end of the process. What might they have found if they looked deeper than the evident allure of a man's speaking ability or his vision to plant a hundred churches? How might a witness for Christ in that community have been saved if they had lingered longer on a man's self-control—on his anger, his lust, or his greed? Every pastor wants to make a difference; we want scores of people to see the excellency of Christ. But sending agencies and church-planting churches need to be more careful to emphasize what Scripture emphasizes.

I've been in Washington, DC, now for over fourteen years. I've seen planters arrive and thrive, and I've seen them arrive and flame out. More often than not, the ones who thrive *do* have charisma, but their charisma doesn't shine as bright as their love for Christ, his people, and their surrounding community. Shiny charisma might attract people on the front end, but it rarely endures.

Long Obedience in the Same Direction

The late Eugene Peterson summarized the Christian life as a "long obedience in the same direction." In his book by the same name, he writes provocatively and, in my experience, prophetically:

> It is not difficult in such a world to get a person interested in the message of the gospel; it is terrifically difficult to sustain the interest. Millions of people in our culture make decisions for Christ, but there is a dreadful attrition rate. Many claim to have been born again, but evidence for mature Christian discipleship is slim. In our kind of culture anything, even news about God, can be sold if it is packaged freshly; but when it loses its novelty, it goes on the garbage heap. There is a great market for religious experience in our world; there is little enthusiasm for the patient acquisition of virtue, little inclination to sign up for a long apprenticeship in what earlier generations of Christians called holiness.[3]

Peterson is just repeating what Paul said to Timothy. And what Peter said to the Dispersion (1 Pet. 1:1). And what God is saying

---

3 Eugene H. Peterson, *A Long Obedience in the Same Direction: Discipleship in an Instant Society* (InterVarsity Press, 2000), 16.

to us. The power is in the gospel, God's word, and the Spirit. Our churches need to be filled with men and women who believe this. Our churches need to be led by pastors who believe this.

A magnetic personality and eloquent composure are wonderful gifts to have. But they're bonus, extra, unnecessary. They're chia seeds and whey protein.

Planting churches for the glory of Christ and the good of his people is tough work. But if we emphasize what the Lord emphasizes, then no matter what happens, we can rest easy.

"Boring" Preaching

A few months after making his "boring" comment, the brother and his family left our church. Thankfully, they joined another gospel-loving church. But to my great surprise, others in that initial community group stayed—and they still show up every Sunday. I remain grateful.

In fact, I recently scrolled through the contacts on my phone. I came across names I added years ago and never deleted, like Paul, a college student I ran into on the Metro platform. We started talking about the Bible, and he came to our group soon after. He left DC to join and eventually become an elder in a church plant in Brooklyn. And Vaughn, a lost soul who, in God's strange providence, wound up at our services and in my office more times than I can count. Jodie, the Vanderbilt grad, kept coming back and eventually met her husband at our church. Josh and Dan and Flower—each surrendered their lives to Christ.

These folks endured my boring preaching. Some of them still endure it! Why? Because as I opened and explained and applied God's word, they smelled the aroma of life—not only from the pulpit but over meals in restaurants and during walks around the block.

And yet, as I scrolled through these names, I noticed a few who didn't endure. I need to pray for them, and check in on some.

As I think about all of these precious people, my mind goes back to where we met and how. I think about conversations we had and prayers we prayed. Tears fill my eyes as I think about how the Lord used simple men who were spurred on by God's extraordinary gospel to love others, and to keep loving them.

If we are going to plant churches full of people who treasure Christ together, then we need pastors who are marked by character, not charisma. Imagine what God might have planned for the good of our neighbors and the nations! Faithfulness may not be flashy, and it might look quite boring. But it leads to fruitfulness—every time.

4

Church, Not Crowd

The Markers of the Planter

OVER TIME, our little gathering in my apartment got more and more uncomfortable; we ran out of places for people to sit. I preached in the same living room where hours before I was eating popcorn and watching football. Since we didn't put my home address on our website or handouts, people had to email us to find out where we were, and only then would we tell them. Most of the people who came, though, we'd already met beforehand.

We figured it was time to find some public space, so we rented a local community center that people could never seem to find. (Some free advice: rent places people can find!) Someone had to stand at the doors because they stayed locked. Show up late? Locked out! If you made it in, you'd sit down in one of the thirty or so chairs we set out just before the service.

Before covenanting as a church, we wanted people to understand what a church is and what a church does. So we took a couple months to preach on the church. Only after doing this did we open up the possibility of joining the church we said all along we planned to begin.

In addition to the four of us—us two church planters and our long-suffering wives—we received sixteen requests to join. We sat down with each person and talked about all we had been learning together: the gospel, the Bible, evangelism, discipleship, the church, and more. Because there were so few of us, these conversations were easy, natural, and even fun.

Fourteen of those sixteen eventually joined the church. The other two, whom you'll meet in the next chapter, decided to delay.

And then, on March 28, 2010, Restoration Church covenanted together—all eighteen of us. Oh, the joy!

A local Baptist church allowed us to use its facility for the service. Two pastors who had been instrumental to us flew in to participate. One of them preached, and the other led the service. All our prospective members stood and answered a series of questions in solidarity. After doing so, we took the Lord's Supper together for the first time. Two sisters were baptized outside the building in a mobile baptismal—the church's baptismal was somehow broken!—and in less than a year from our arrival, though we knew absolutely no one beforehand, Restoration Church was no longer our dream but our reality.

The Pattern of the Apostles

Why were we so careful? Why did we go through interviews and months of teaching before we started this thing called a church? In short, we did what we did because we were trying to follow the pattern of the New Testament. In Matthew 28:18–20, Jesus commissions his disciples to make disciples, baptize them, and teach them to observe all he commanded. The apostles obeyed Jesus's command not by gathering crowds and teaching them, but by intentionally forming and organizing local churches. Take a look.

Jesus tells his apostles that they ought to be his witnesses in the world (Acts 1:8). Almost immediately, Peter preaches the gospel in Jerusalem (Acts 2:14–36), and some respond in faith. They ask, "What should we do to be saved?" To which Peter responds, remembering what Jesus told him, "Repent and be baptized" (Acts 2:38). Luke summarizes the events like this: "So those who received his word were baptized, and there were added that day about three thousand souls" (Acts 2:41).

Clearly, the apostles understood that repentant believers should be baptized and, upon their baptism, they should be added to a church.

What comes after that? Gratefully, Acts 2:42–47 paints a picture of the first church. They regularly gathered (2:46), devoted themselves to the apostles' teaching, broke bread (the Lord's Supper), and prayed (2:42). As they were together, they praised God and experienced favor among all the people (2:44, 47).

We see something similar in Acts 4:32–37. And in Acts 11, God's people scatter in the face of opposition. Many flee to Antioch. When they get there, what do they do? They preach the gospel to those outside the kingdom and then form a church (11:20, 25–26).

On Paul's missionary journeys, he repeats the same practice time and again: he goes into a city, he preaches the gospel, and he forms local churches. He does this in Antioch in Pisidia (Acts 13:14–44), Iconium, and Lystra (Acts 14:21–23). Upon his arrival back home in Antioch, he gathers the church together to report on his work (Acts 14:27). The Jerusalem Council features representatives of local churches (Acts 15:3–4). Paul begins churches in Corinth (1 Cor.

1:1–2), Ephesus (Eph. 1:1), and Thessalonica (1 Thess. 1:1), just to name a few.

But what exactly *is* a church? How do we know that Paul planted a church? After all, if we're going to "plant churches," we should probably know what a church is and what a church does. Right?

What Is a Church?

The church is the beloved bride of Christ (2 Cor. 11:2; Eph. 5:25–27; Rev. 19:7–9). Each visible local church is an expression of the invisible universal church that Jesus purchased with his own blood (Acts 20:28). Though the visible expressions of our churches may be small, awkward, and ravaged with sin and struggle, she is the delight of her heavenly husband. What God said of his people Israel might surely be said of the church: "You are precious in my eyes, and honored, and I love you" (Isa. 43:4).

The Protestant Reformers—Luther, Zwingli, and Calvin—defined the local church by directing us to the handling of the gospel. Here's how Calvin put it: "Wherever we see the word of God purely preached and heard, and the sacraments administered according to Christ's institution, there, it is not to be doubted, a church of God exists."[1] More recently, theologian Jonathan Leeman defined the church as "a group of Christians who regularly gather in Christ's name to officially affirm and oversee one another's membership in Jesus Christ and his kingdom through gospel preaching and gospel ordinances."[2]

---

1 John Calvin, *Institutes of the Christian Religion*, ed. Henry Beveridge (Peabody, MA: Hendrickson, 2008), 4.1.9.

2 Jonathan Leeman, "What Is a Local Church?," 9Marks, accessed September 1, 2022, https://www.9marks.org.

I like those definitions. Here's the shorthand definition I use: "A local church is the regular assembly of Christians who have covenanted together in order to preach the gospel, portray the gospel, and protect the gospel."

Let me explain what I mean. Churches must preach God's word and show their listeners every week how it centers on the person and work of Christ. When I say churches "portray the gospel," I mean they carefully "administer"—to use Calvin's word—baptism and the Lord's Supper. By "protect the gospel," I'm referring to the work of marking off Christians from the world so as to "bind and loose" people on earth as it is in heaven (Matt. 16:19). In other words, I'm referring to church membership and discipline.

When these three elements are faithfully practiced among a regular assembly of Christians, then you have the basic elements that constitute a church. There's more that a church does, of course, but these are its basic ingredients.

Definition Helps Mission

I wanted to write this book because I can't help but notice the absence of the *church* in most *church-planting* resources. I've read more than a dozen books on church planting. I've watched talks online. I've read blog posts, I've listened to podcasts, and I've attended conferences and assessments. I've talked with "strategists," and I've met with future planters. And you know what? Ecclesiology is hardly mentioned!

Why is that? It seems that some people believe that the more definition and oversight you bring to the church, the more you will quiet the evangelistic thrust of the church.

My good friend Joel Kurz thought this way at one point. Joel is a pastor in West Baltimore. He planted the Garden Church a decade ago. I was talking to him recently, and he said something that fascinated me: "I thought that if we defined terms and actually used our statement of faith, we would keep people from coming— or we would be less likely to go to our neighbors with the gospel. Turns out, it was the opposite."

He started his church plant with few definitions or expectations in place—no statement of faith that members had to agree on, no membership process, no clear teaching on the church. He said that over time their church became "theologically fuzzy, ecclesiologically squishy, and morally ambiguous." Division grew. Their lack of clarity became a heavy burden.

What did Joel do to try to fix this? He sought to bring clarity through two oft-overlooked documents: a statement of faith and a church covenant. He used these to foster theological unity and biblical community, which in turn has fueled the congregation's sense of its mission.[3]

As we noted in chapter 2, church-planting resources usually emphasize size, speed, self-sufficiency, and spread. These measures of success are all admirable and even desirable, but by themselves they fail to guide planters to know if they've accomplished what they set out to do: plant a church.

It's tempting to be vague; it's tempting to keep the fences low and the doors open so that anyone can come in and stay a while. But as Joel learned—and as many church planters have learned—such instincts can rather quickly hinder the mission of the church.

But let's get practical. How might clear definitions actually show love for people, strengthen the mission of the church, and honor

---

3 Joel Kurz, "Church Planters, Don't Wait to Put Your Documents in Place!," 9Marks, accessed September 1, 2022, https://www.9marks.org.

Christ? When we preach, portray, and protect the gospel, four beautiful things start to happen.

Benefits of Defining the Work

Meaningful Membership

Imagine trying to play a pick-game of basketball at the local park. No jerseys, just a dozen interested people. What's the best way to start? Divide up the teams! Back in the day, we'd play "shirts and skins." Without teams, you've just got a mass of undefined but interested people. The same is true for the church. Meaningful membership defines the citizens of the kingdom of God here on earth. It clarifies who has been given the "keys to the kingdom of God" and who hasn't.

After Peter makes the first profession of faith in Christ, Jesus tells him,

> You are Peter, and on this rock I will build my church, and the gates of hell shall not prevail against it. I will give you the keys of the kingdom of heaven, and whatever you bind on earth shall be bound in heaven, and whatever you loose on earth shall be loosed in heaven. (Matt. 16:18–19)

Just a few chapters later, Jesus tells us what to do with someone who takes the name of "brother" but sins against you. If the person won't listen to your correction, or the correction of a few, then you are to:

> . . . tell it to the church. And if he refuses to listen even to the church, let him be to you as a Gentile and a tax collector.

Truly, I say to you, whatever you bind on earth shall be bound in heaven, and whatever you loose on earth shall be loosed in heaven. . . . For where two or three are gathered in my name, there am I among them. (Matt. 18:15–18, 20)

This is such a beautiful and humbling task. We have been given the responsibility of defining the body of Christ before the judgment of Christ. Just think about the number of people taking the name of "brother" or "sister" in the world, but whom Jesus "never knew" (Matt. 7:21–23). We fuel the mission by making distinctions as clear as we can through membership.

Pastoral Oversight

In what must be one of the most intimidating verses of the New Testament for a pastor, we read, "Obey your leaders and submit to them, for they are keeping watch over your souls, as those who will have to give an account" (Heb. 13:17).

At the very least, church leaders will give an account for the truth they taught their people (see James 3:1). But that's not all. These leaders also seem to have some kind of meaningful connection to the *individual lives of their people.* After all, these leaders are "keeping watch over your souls." They are overseeing the individual lives of their people. Like Jesus, they know their people and their people know them (John 10:14). Pastors ward off wolves and protect their flocks "so that [they] may no longer be children, tossed to and fro by the waves and carried about by every wind of doctrine, by human cunning" (Eph. 4:14).

Paul sought to establish elders over the churches he planted. Here's how he counseled the elders of the church in Ephesus: "Pay careful attention to yourselves and to all the flock, in which the

Holy Spirit has made you overseers, to care for the church of God, which he obtained with his own blood" (Acts 20:28).

Notice how Paul assumes nearness, intimacy, love, and concern. He assumes these Ephesian shepherds know their flock, their stories and struggles, their wins and losses. Jesus knows his sheep, and his sheep know him (John 10:14). Surely his undershepherds should do the same. Surely he wants his sheep to be cared for. After all, he loved his sheep enough to lay down his life for them. Enough to go after one if he saw him stray (Luke 15:3–5)! That's why we should aim to know the names of our people, not just the numbers.

Living Out the One Anothers

Paul writes to the local church in Corinth, "For just as the body is one and has many members, and all the members of the body, though many, are one body, so it is with Christ. . . . Now you are the body of Christ and individually members of it" (1 Cor. 12:12, 27).

Paul wrote that to the Corinthians, but it just as easily could be applied to your church or mine. The body of Christ is always defined. It's not a formless mass in the digital "cloud," nor is it a nameless crowd. It's a body.

When I look through my membership directory, I see the actual people that I've covenanted with to do all those "one anothers." Isabel, Colleen, Daniel, David, Jodie, Hannah, and Jeron—these are the ones I'm supposed to not neglect meeting together with and encouraging as the day draws near (Heb. 10:25). Just take a moment and read these verses from the perspective of a defined body of believers. Picture these things happening among a people that agreed with one another to do so:

May the God of endurance and encouragement grant you to live in such harmony with *one another*, in accord with Christ Jesus, that together you may with one voice glorify the God and Father of our Lord Jesus Christ. Therefore welcome *one another* as Christ has welcomed you, for the glory of God. (Rom. 15:5–7)

Finally, brothers, rejoice. Aim for restoration, comfort one *another*, agree with *one another*, live in peace; and the God of love and peace will be with you. (2 Cor. 13:11)

Through love serve *one another*. (Gal. 5:13)

But exhort *one another* every day, as long as it is called "today," that none of you may be hardened by the deceitfulness of sin. (Heb. 3:13)

Show hospitality to *one another* without grumbling. (1 Pet. 4:9)

But if we walk in the light, as he is in the light, we have fellowship with *one another*, and the blood of Jesus his Son cleanses us from all sin. (1 John 1:7)

These passages, along with many others, indicate that the church is not like a concert or a pep rally, where individual people stand to receive individual truths to be lived out individually. Instead, the church is more like a human body that needs its different parts to work together toward the end of displaying the excellencies of Christ. I'll sometimes say from the pulpit, "You can't eat Momma's cooking and not expect to help clean the dishes. This ain't Jiffy Lube. We have to love one another and not just be individually serviced." As we love one another, as we preach and portray the gospel, we literally fulfill the missionary task that Jesus designed for us (John 13:35).

The Glory of the Church

In Acts 12:1 we read, "About that time Herod the king laid violent hands on some who belonged to the church." Think about that for a second. How did Herod know *who belonged to the church*? Certainly they would have been known to gather regularly. But there was more. To belong to the church is to belong to a definable community (which Herod saw as a threat). This definable community is known to God, one another, and its leaders. And it participates in the two gospel ordinances and sacrificial love toward their neighbors in Jesus's name.

You might say this is the glory of the church. Jesus prayed to his Father before going to the cross: "I am praying for them. I am not praying for the world but for those whom you have given me, for they are yours. All mine are yours, and yours are mine, and I am glorified in them" (John 17:9–10).

The Father and the Son know their own. Jesus prayed for us. He died for us. He still prays for us. He is glorified in us. Everything we do as a church either enhances or detracts from our reflecting Jesus to a watching world (Eph. 3:10).

So we need to make the church's mission clear. Not only will that make your job as a pastor clearer, but it will also help the body to grow in maturity and stability. As we do so, those who don't know Christ will see his church and long to know more. They will abandon the chase for fleeting glories and long to take up the glory promised to God's people by Jesus himself. They will walk your aisles and rise up from your baptismal pools and eat at your

Communion tables and serve the poor because they met Jesus, the King of glory, when they met his wife, the church.

Installation

Our covenanting ceremony was both celebratory and solemn.

That night, Joey and I stood up as the sixteen other freshly minted members sat down behind us. Our visiting pastor friends asked us a series of critical questions about our convictions and our willingness to step down if we gave up those convictions. We agreed. They then asked us if we would care for the flock that God had purchased at the cost of his only Son. We said yes. We then sat down as the members behind us stood up. It was now their turn to answer some questions.

For the rest of my life, I will never forget what happened next. I'd never been a pastor before. I had taught Sunday school, led a community group, discipled people, preached sermons, and finished a master of divinity. But I'd never been a pastor. Then my pastoral example from younger days asked these people, "Will you promise to submit to Joey and Nathan as your pastors as they submit to the Lord?" Their response broke me: *yes*, they said in unison. Tears streamed down my face.

After the service, each of us came forward and signed our names to the handwritten covenant that still hangs where we gather every week. We were a motley crew: a handful of students, a couple stay-at-home moms, some military folks, a project manager, a nanny, a teacher, and two incredibly green pastors. And yet, despite our differences and uncertainty, we covenanted together to love God and neighbor. It was a simple affair. It didn't make the news here on the earth, but I'm confident the angels sang—and the demons plotted. A new embassy of the kingdom was raised up for the glory of Christ.

5

Unexplainable, Not Explainable

The Culture of the Planter

"STREET SENSE! Two dollars. Help the homeless!"

Tyrone Murray was a force. He stood about 6'2" and weighed about 260 pounds. In his midfifties, his booming voice would have rivaled George Whitefield's. In a fluorescent green vest, he sat on a milk crate under a Best Buy sign at the top of the Tenleytown Metro stop. He would speak to every (and I mean *every*) passerby and ask for a couple of bucks to buy a newspaper written by the homeless. The goal was to make enough money each day to buy a meal and a hotel room on the opposite side of town.

Sitting next to him was Edna, Tyrone's opposite. She was shorter and quieter than her confidant. She donned a large straw hat to shield the sun. When she wasn't running errands for Tyrone, she sat quietly, often chuckling as her husband made some cheeky comment.

I was introduced to Tyrone and Edna early on in my arrival to the city. They were hard to miss, and in those days I was looking for anyone to listen to me; I'd begun to realize that strangers not only don't talk to one another on the streets of Northwest DC, but they don't even look at one another. So here was my chance to tell someone about Jesus!

After introducing myself, Tyrone wanted to know why I moved to the city. To plant a church, I said. To my surprise, he was interested. He told me that when we started gathering, I should let them know.

Joey usually picked up Tyrone and Edna and brought them to our apartment for Bible study. Every single week, they were ready to go. They'd sit in the same chairs of our living room, holding court, it seemed. The room was young, mostly white. So they stood out. Not to mention, neither of them understood the gospel. In the eyes of the world, Edna and Tyrone didn't seem to fit; but then again, none of us "fit" into the gospel.

Unexplainable

"For Jews demand signs and Greeks seek wisdom, but we preach Christ crucified" (1 Cor. 1:22–23). When it comes to faith, the world looks for something understandable, something reasonable before it will jump in. The Jews wanted Jesus to perform some dog-and-pony tricks before they would commit to follow him. The Greeks wanted to weigh the logical evidence of his kingdom, and then they'd follow. But Paul comes in and says both are wrong; we preach about a Savior who refused to offer a sign save that of Jonah (Luke 11:29), one who lost in order to win (Gal. 3:13).

Upside-Down Kingdom

This topsy-turvy kingdom has always been the way the Lord has worked. He chose barren women to be the forebearers of an entire nation (Gen. 11:30; 25:21; 29:31). He made it a point to highlight Israel's insignificance as a reason for the Lord's choosing (Deut. 7:7). The mighty nation of Egypt was overcome by plagues and a wall of water, all of which were miracles done by the Lord, not accomplished by Israel (Ex. 20:2). Even the conquest of Canaan is unexplainable apart from the Lord going before Israel and driving out their enemies. I mean, Jericho was conquered by walking around a wall and blowing some horns! Not exactly elements of great force and intimidation.

This pattern doesn't change when Jesus, the King of kings, comes on the scene. He's born to a betrothed teenage virgin from Nazareth. His cousin John prepared for his ministry by going out in the wilderness and preaching in a hair shirt, eating locusts, and calling people to take responsibility for their own rebellion. Jesus was not only palace-less but homeless. His preaching was as likely to push crowds *away* as it was to attract the masses. This could have had something to do with his message: "Take up your electric chair, hate Mom and Dad, and leave 'em to be buried by someone else." He was crucified by his own people and his disciples ran off and left him in his darkest hour. Before the resurrection, few souls still hoped in Christ, and they were basically all scared stiff and wondering what to do next (Acts 1:15).

A Better City

The gospel message is fundamentally about another world. When we preach, we invite in the aroma of *another* city, a *better* city than this one (Heb. 11:10). In this city, all tribes, peoples, and languages gather together as one (Rev. 7:9). There is no Jew or Greek, no slave or free, no male and female, because they are all one in Christ Jesus (Gal. 3:28). The population of this city finds its supreme treasure in Christ the Lord (Matt. 13:44–46), the one who loved them enough to lay his own life down so that we might know life and have it abundantly in him (John 10:10).

We are exiles and sojourners in this land (1 Pet. 2:11). As this prayer from *Valley of Vision* says, "Ours is a kingdom where the way down is the way up, to be low is to be high, to give is to receive, to bear the cross is to wear the crown."[1]

We don't go from good to great by learning how to be strong in the eyes of the world, but by learning to embrace our weakness. We don't seek our best life now, but our best life there, in our heavenly home. We don't embrace self-help, but God's help for daily bread. We don't expect quick profits, but painful toil. We are in the wilderness, but soon enough we will get to the Jordan and cross over into the new Canaan.

We love enemies and forgive as we have been forgiven. We are a people of grace, love, and mercy. We are a people unexplainable apart from the reality of Christ our Lord and supreme treasure.

Target Groups

Early in our church-planting efforts, one of our supporting organizations required Joey and me to attend some training events. On one occasion, we were told to write down our "target group." The idea was to identify a common interest group in our community so that we could design our plant to be more attractive to them—families, college students, young professionals, and so on. If we could identify our target group and focus our efforts there, then our church would grow more quickly, because the majority of people would already have something in common.

---

1 Arthur Bennett, *The Valley of Vision: A Collection of Puritan Prayers & Devotions* (Edinburgh: Banner of Truth Trust, 1975), xxiv.

When the kindhearted and well-intentioned instructor came to our table, Joey and I sat there doing nothing. He asked why we weren't participating; we said we have no intention of choosing a target group. "We're targeting anyone who speaks English, and maybe even a few who don't." Later, we were told that this instructor "didn't understand" what we were trying to do.

In their book *Compelling Community*, Mark Dever and Jamie Dunlop document what they call "Gospel Plus" factors that serve to build churches on something in addition to the gospel:

Similar life experience: Singles groups, newly married Bible studies, and young professionals networks build community based on demographic groupings.

Similar identity: Cowboy churches, motorcycle churches, arts churches, and the like are all gospel-believing churches with something other than the gospel at the core of their identity.

Similar cause: Ministry teams for feeding the hungry, helping an elementary school, and combating human trafficking build community based on shared passion for a God-honoring cause.

Similar needs: Program-based churches build community by assembling people into programs based on the similarity of their felt needs.

Similar social position: Sometimes a ministry—or an entire church—gathers the "movers and shakers" of society.[2]

None of these things are wrong in and of themselves. But if our core strategy is to find something other than the gospel to "grow"

---

2 Mark Dever and Jamie Dunlop, *The Compelling Community: Where God's Power Makes a Church Attractive* (Wheaton, IL: Crossway, 2015), 21.

our church, then we're doing it all wrong. The uniqueness of the church is its expression of God's "manifold wisdom" (Eph. 3:10). Each person with his or her myriad of backgrounds and experiences collected together as one united family in Christ is unlike anything else in all the world. Neither the United Nations nor the diverse fanbase of a sports team can compare to the expression of God's wisdom that makes up the church.

If we learn to love what God loves and who God loves more than we love achieving size at a quick speed for the ends of financial sufficiency and spread—if we learn to focus on names, not numbers—then we would build on more solid foundations. Christ and his kingdom would be more manifestly exhibited and, in the process, we might convince an increasingly divided world that the city they are looking for is real.

One Imperfect Example

How did we seek to build our church around Christ and his gospel over everything else?

First, in an effort to engage young and old, American and African, married and single, white and black, we chose to sing congregationally. Many traditions are familiar with this kind of singing. I've been to the Caribbean, South Asia, Europe, and Central Asia, and all of them sing different songs with different beats, but they all sing congregationally. We also chose to sing both new and old songs. This grabs different age ranges, and occasionally encourages both groups to yield their preferences to another.

Second, we chose to preach expositionally. More than that, I sought to preach simple enough to engage both the homeless and the highly educated. This may seem impossible, but it's not. It's possible to explain deep truths clearly while not compromising the truth. Many children's books do this well; most preachers just need some more practice.

Third, we chose to feature many preachers, not just one. Though I was paid to serve as the main preaching pastor, I didn't preach every single week. We didn't want our people to get too attached to a particular personality in the pulpit. So I preached about three weeks of the month and Joey would preach the fourth. As we added elders, we had them preach as they were able in addition to bringing in other faithful men from different backgrounds. I also sought to use illustrations and applications that addressed the weary parent, the stressed-out student, the disenfranchised minority, the nonbeliever, the older saint, the younger saint, the man, and the woman.

Obviously, no matter how hard you try, you will face limitations. The very fact that we sing, preach, and pray only in English is a natural barrier. Likewise, some people would rather have loud music and others would rather we not pray so much. But ultimately, our decisions were grounded in the desire to love all our community with all of the gospel. Because we did, all kinds of people have found a home with us. Not because we've figured out some "proven strategy," but because they were drawn by a Jesus that was big enough to be trusted, together as a family as we loved one another like family.

All Kinds of Names, Not One Kind of Number

Had we never taken this approach, quite frankly, I probably would have excused myself from building a relationship with Tyrone and Edna. They were nothing like me. Our experiences were almost entirely the opposite. They grew up in poverty; I grew up in privilege. They had very little education; I had more than enough education. They weren't going to offer much for our bottom line, and they certainly wouldn't make people comfortable, as evidenced by the hundreds of people who walked by them every day. But we stayed with them. Better yet, they stayed with us. They were patient with our failures. And after a while, those two precious people gave their lives to Christ.

Tyrone would sit on the front row every week as the church grew. He and Edna would rarely miss. He would interact with the sermons (go online and listen in—you'll hear him in the background). He would sing beautifully. He would interact with Ivy League PhDs. He and Edna were family. They served us and we served them.

Inexplicable Grief

Then one night I received one of those phone calls that every pastor dreads. Tyrone had a heart attack and didn't make it. Edna called, all alone, from the hospital. We rushed over and held her for what seemed like hours—weeping, groaning, switching between prayers and silence.

In the eyes of the hospital staff, our shared lives made no sense. Why were two young white dudes from Ward 3 of Washington, DC, so grief-stricken with a middle-aged, poor black woman from Southeast DC? Why were *we* the first phone call?

Our church was so brokenhearted by the loss of our brother that we hosted a community-wide memorial. Since Tyrone had been in that spot at Tenleytown for so long, talking to so many people, we put a notice up for all to come. That room was packed with lawyers, students, and homeless folks. We told some stories, prayed, and sang. I stood up as his pastor and preached the gospel. It was a beautiful time together.

On the way out that night, one young man pulled me aside and asked about our church. I told him a bit and gave him a card.

About six months later, that man and his wife were standing in the baptismal waters at our church, bearing testimony to how Christ had found and rescued them. Tyrone's death had led to their life in Christ and they, along with their young daughter, are still with us today.

Brothers and sisters, let's plant churches that are unexplainable apart from the gospel. Yes, such work may go slower and be harder—and church-planting strategists may find your approach odd. But I assure you: heaven won't.

6

Christ, Not You

The Goal of a Planter

I HAD ENOUGH self-control to hide it, but in those first years of planting I was quite vain. The vanity wasn't always conscious. Yet underneath the surface, I thought we were something special since we were planting a church in Washington, DC. I believed our story deserved to be told in interviews with Christian publications. It was 2008, and the urban church-planting buzz was all the rage. And we were doing it!

We would occasionally attend gatherings of church planters, and I walked into those rooms smug. I'd introduce myself to a brother and ask about his work. He'd share all the ways he was giving his life for Jesus in a smaller city. Internally, I was measuring him up and thinking of myself as better than him. I was wrong!

Thankfully, I didn't get access to the limelight I wanted. But my vanity still made its way into our church plant. Every time something good would happen, I would shout it out on social media in order to "ask for prayer." On our monthly update videos,

I would list all the good things in order to "give praise to God." Meanwhile, I never mentioned how bad my preaching was and how some people had left because of it.

I don't have many regrets about much of what we did in planting, but I do have plenty of regrets about my desires. I needed the plant to be healthy because I needed to be seen as a healthy planting pastor. I wanted to be praised. To make matters worse, I was glad to have other churches planted in DC, but I didn't want them to succeed *quite* as much as mine.

To reflect back on all this is embarrassing. Yet worse than my embarrassment now was my sin then.

History is riddled with influential people wrecking lives in the name of Jesus. We would be fools to think we were above this possibility. The sooner we confess deep down in our hearts that church planting is not about us, the sooner we'll be ready to do some really good work. You might agree with this in principle, but you've got to know it deep down. Church planting is not about building our platforms, reputations, or visions for the community. It's about holding high the excellencies of Christ. Church planting is not about you; it's about him. Churches exist to exalt Christ, not a pastor or a particular philosophy of ministry.

Let's take some time to consider why we are planting churches to begin with.

The Arc of Creation

I like to have a handful of verses memorized to meditate on and employ in common pastoral situations. One of those verses is John 5:39: "You search the Scriptures because you think that in them you have eternal life; and it is they that bear witness about me."

I love this passage because in a single sentence Jesus makes an important point: "The Bible is about me!"

Before his coming, the Father promised to send one who would crush sin and death (Gen. 3:15), who would be in the line of Abraham (Gen. 12:3) and David (2 Sam. 7:12). He would be born of a virgin (Isa. 7:14) to comfort God's people (Isa. 40:1) by his substitutionary atonement for sin (Isa. 53), purchasing an everlasting covenant never to be broken (Ezek. 37:26–27).

The New Testament begins with the birth certificate and credentials of Jesus as the Christ (Matt. 1:1–17). It carries on with story after story of the power, majesty, and beauty of Christ. Jesus ultimately purchases the church, his wife, by his own blood (Acts 20:28; Eph. 5:22–32). The epistles reflect on Christ who *is* our life (Col. 3:4), as well as document what it looks like to "walk in love *as* Christ loved us" (Eph. 5:1).

When we come to the end of the Bible, we find a congregation too great to number from all tribes, peoples, and languages, enjoying the infinite worth of Christ together as one (Rev. 5:9; 7:9). The final two verses of Scripture feature Jesus saying he is coming soon, the church asking him to come, and the benediction of his blessing to be with us all as we wait (Rev. 22:20–21).

The glory of Christ is the aim of the universe. Therefore, our lives and churches must be saturated with the glory of Christ and not a hint of anything else. When we win people, we must unmistakably win them with Jesus, to Jesus, and for Jesus—not our personalities, visions, or glory.

Stated Belief + Actual Practice = Actual Belief

You wouldn't have picked up this book if you didn't agree at least in principle about the arc of creation. The problem comes when we aren't conscious or honest about the real reasons we plant churches. I *professed* to plant churches for the glory of Christ, but my *practice* had a lurking desire that compromised our work. I wanted glory.

When I was at Southeastern Baptist Theological Seminary, professor Mark Liederbach happened to also be one of my pastors at North Wake Church. He ingrained a formula into my DNA that I'll never forget: Stated Belief + Actual Practice = Actual Belief.

It's not enough to *state* that your church plant exists for the glory of Christ; your church practices will reveal your *actual* belief. As Calvin teaches, our hearts are idol factories. Hovering below the surface is a temptation we must recognize. This desire might never be named, but you can spot it in the way a church plant goes about its ministry. Here are a couple ways to evaluate whether your plant is being built on the glory of Christ or the glory of you and your vision.

Identity

In his book *Dangerous Calling*, Paul Tripp says, "Either you will be getting your identity vertically, from who you are in Christ, or you will be shopping for it horizontally in the situations, experiences, and relationships of your daily life."[1] Far too many pastors know enough of the right answers to play the game of external Christianity, when below the surface they're doing ministry to satisfy an itch to be affirmed, accepted, and maybe even heralded. Church planting makes these base desires easy to attain since you write the rules from the beginning.

If you're planting to satisfy your desire to be liked, followed, or heard, repent! If you're planting to gain a large enough following to

1   Paul David Tripp, *Dangerous Calling* (Wheaton, IL: Crossway, 2012), 22.

get book contracts or places on certain stages, confess your sin. If you're planting in order to multiply so that you will be seen as the next church-planting guru, pray for God to sanctify your desires. Such aspirations attempt to steal from the infinite glory of Christ. Plus, you'll never find in church planting what you're looking for. The work is too hard, and the paybacks never match the aspirations, because they weren't designed to.

Don't plant a church to form an identity. Plant a church to make Christ's identity more clear to more people so that *he* might receive glory, not you.

Form of Godliness

Paul sounds another alarm that may describe many church planters. Consider his counsel to Timothy:

> But understand this, that in the last days there will come times of difficulty. For people will be lovers of self, lovers of money, proud, arrogant, abusive, disobedient to their parents, ungrateful, unholy, heartless, unappeasable, slanderous, without self-control, brutal, not loving good, treacherous, reckless, swollen with conceit, lovers of pleasure rather than lovers of God, having the appearance of godliness, but denying its power. Avoid such people. For among them are those who creep into households and capture weak women, burdened with sins and led astray by various passions, always learning and never able to arrive at a knowledge of the truth. (2 Tim. 3:1–7)

Two things stick out: "having the *appearance* of godliness but denying its power" and "always learning and never able to arrive at a knowledge of the truth." These two things describe church planting that minors on clear biblical teaching, as evidenced by the neglect of hard doctrines in favor of "relevance" to "reach" more people.

In these kinds of churches, it's possible to find a statement of faith buried somewhere and, upon reading it, it probably says all the right things. But in the life of the church those truths are largely unknown and undefined. There's no systematic teaching of those doctrines to a definable group of people week in and out. This lack reveals an interest in something else. That something else could be building a platform for a personality in the pulpit, or making that church's name known in the neighborhood, or trumpeting a countercultural philosophy of ministry. Whatever it is, it takes the *form* of godliness. But by rallying a crowd around something other than the excellency of Christ, you deny the power of Christ.

Our communities don't need entertainment and affirmation centers with a little Jesus-driven life change here and there. Communities need churches that will love them enough to tell them the truth about Christ and his gospel. They need a church that will not have a form of godliness, but actual godliness. Make it clear to yourself and to your community that you unequivocally exist to magnify Christ, and no other.

Treasuring Christ Together

What does it look like to plant a church that treasures Christ together?

Evangelizing the Glory of Christ

A well-intentioned, well-known Christian athlete shared the gospel with some students at a nearby university. He said that winning national championships was fun, but those wins still left him empty. When he heard the gospel and found the truth in Jesus, he trusted Christ and was born again. Since then, he's understood what it means to be fulfilled. After this he called the students in the room to do the same, to come to Jesus so that they might find the answer to their hungers.

I've heard that presentation of the gospel more times than I can count. I'm confident I've *given* that presentation more times than I can count. It's not as though the content of the athlete's message was wrong. The problem was his emphasis on personal fulfillment. He'd found his purpose. Yes and amen. But the reality is, this dear brother left people with a gospel and a Jesus that sounded like another spiritual philosophy that could "complete" them. They didn't hear a gospel that called them to repent of their sins, die to themselves, and worship the risen Christ for his eternal praise and their eternal good.

We'll talk more about evangelism later, but when sharing the gospel, don't hide from the reality of our position before a holy God. Speak about our sin in a way that captures the depth of our darkness. Then, pull out the light of Christ. Tell people how Christ bore their sin on the cross and triumphed over it in the resurrection. Not only that, tell them the goal of their life is, in fact, purpose and pleasure. But the only lasting purpose and pleasure is found in knowing and enjoying Christ forever.

When you pray, teach, and practice evangelism, make sure the praise and enjoyment of Christ is at the center of the call. Don't use the gospel as a philosophy. Use the gospel as a call to worship! More him, less you.

Preaching the Glory of Christ

When hanging out with Christians, I often ask two questions: Are you glad you're a Christian? Assuming they answer yes, I ask a follow-up: "Why?"

People's faces light up when I ask that. It's like you're asking me why I love to be married to my wife, or why I love pancakes, baseball, or hiking through Glacier National Park. I could give you a thousand reasons, and you're asking me to tell you about it. That's the way our preaching ought to be.

When we preach, we should not only look for pathways to Christ's death, burial, resurrection, and ascension. We also need to show the heart behind these wonderful realities so people will regularly be reminded of *why* it's good to follow Jesus—why he's trustworthy, good, faithful, just, loving, and patient. In your preaching, don't just tell people the gospel; tell them *why* Jesus is worth following and laying our lives down for. Give people a reason to smile and be glad they've chosen to die to themselves and take up the hard road in order to follow Christ.

Singing the Glory of Christ

Pastoring in the District of Columbia has afforded us the opportunity to minister to people from all over the world. Many are attending a Christian service for the first time. Inevitably, when I ask them what struck them, they tell me it's the singing—not the music, the *singing*.

Singing Christ-exalting songs in congregational unity is a unique joy. We gather every week to be reoriented around our hope and eternal joy. If we can't hear each other sing, or if we sing songs that have more to do with us than Jesus, then our hearts stay out of tune. But if we turn the volume on the instruments down, then the volume on the redeemed will turn up. If we tune the lyrics to frequently remind ourselves of Christ's person and work, our hearts will be returned to what we'll do for an eternity—see and savor the glory of Christ.

Praying the Glory of Christ

Often, prayer in the life of the church is like the fade feature of a movie; it just reorients us to the next scene.

Our church has sought to inject short, medium, and long prayers that make much of Christ all through our life together. We pray publicly and privately that Christ would be exalted in our community groups. We ask the Lord to display the worth of Christ in our preaching. We spend time in our elders' meetings praying for members to live for the glory of Christ more than the glory of their careers. John Onwuchekwa has helpfully taught that praying is like breathing for the Christian.[2] Therefore, when you breathe, make sure you're breathing in a way that exhales the greatness of the glory of God in Christ.

Ordinances for the Glory of Christ

Baptism and the Lord's Supper are the two gifts of the church whose sole intent is to orient us to the work and worth of Christ. Just as the law ordained the Passover meal to remind the forgetful Israelites of who they were and how they came to be, so the ordinances are meant to do the same for us in the church.

So we seize the opportunity in baptisms to explain not only what baptism is but also how it points to the work and worth of Christ. We encourage the baptismal candidate to explain why he or she desires to be baptized and why Jesus is worth living and dying for.

Likewise, when we take the Supper, we not only explain what the bread and wine signify, but we also explain who and what sort of Jesus would do this! We show our people that, soon enough, we

2 John Onwuchekwa, *Prayer: How Praying Together Shapes the Church* (Wheaton, IL: Crossway, 2018), 17.

will eat this meal with him at the marriage supper of the Lamb, where we will finally see him whom our soul loves. This helps turn eyes from self to Savior.

Freedom

As time went on and the Lord was merciful to me, I began to have more genuine desires for the Lord's glory and not my own. I began to notice a shift toward genuine joy when baptismal testimonies stopped referencing my name and started to be more clear on the name of Christ. When people stopped talking about my preaching prowess and started commenting on the beauty of Christ. When I stopped seeking any limelight and, instead, enjoyed walking in the light myself. The freedom of knowing and enjoying Christ together as a church became like air to me.

If you get nothing out of this book, I hope you get this much: we were made to behold the glory of Christ (2 Cor. 3:18). All the ecclesiology and pastoral instructions aim toward that goal. They are prongs holding up the diamond of our precious Savior and friend, Jesus the Christ.

Prince of Peace and Lord of lords
Alpha and Omega
Wonderful Counselor
Mighty God
Friend of sinners
Son of Abraham, Son of David, Son of Man, Son of God
King of the kingdom of heaven
Author and perfector of our faith
Bridegroom
Good shepherd

Great high priest
Immanuel
Lamb of God
Light of the world
The way, the truth, and the life
Our rock and our Redeemer

Let's plant churches that plant churches that plant churches who aim at names, not numbers, so that more and more people might treasure Christ together, forever.

PART 2

CHURCH-PLANTING MOBILIZATION

My family moved to Washington, DC, on May 1, 2009. Joey still needed to finish some classes at seminary, and we needed to raise more money. But he, along with some others, helped us move into our apartment. The Crafts would move to DC about four months later.

Other than a couple of friendly pastors, we didn't know a single person in the city. Not one. So we were instructed to take a month and get situated before beginning any kind of initiative (this was wise advice).

I needed to make some extra money, so I applied for part-time work at every Starbucks within biking distance. My first stop was on the campus of American University, where I saw a young student sitting by himself. I was so amped to start our church that I walked right up to him, sat down, and began to talk. He was from Jordan, and when I asked him if he had ever heard how Christians believe we get to heaven, he said no. I then asked him if I could share the good news with him, and he said yes. After sharing the gospel, I invited him to follow Jesus. That was my very first church-planting conversation in the city. I didn't just pedal to the next Starbucks; I flew!

People like this student were who we came to meet, and we needed a plan for how we could all gather and grow together. Our theology and methodology needed to have some practicality. So must yours.

We've considered the foundational elements of what a church is and does and what a pastor is and does. We'll now consider mobilizing this work.

7

Sent and Sustained by a Church, Not a Parachurch

The Mother of the Planter

LONG BEFORE JOEY AND I moved to Washington, DC, we, along with our families, unknowingly made one of the best decisions for our future church plant. We joined a local church and became active members.

North Wake Church sits in the shadow of Southeastern Baptist Theological Seminary. It was a church plant back in the early 1990s. It started in a house and then eventually moved to a funeral parlor before finally building a structure that looks like a cross between an office building and one of those cool coffee shops full of retro light bulbs. The preaching pastor, Larry Trotter, was the opposite of everything I'd learned to expect from a preacher. I was used to powerful pulpiteers, alliteration, and strong personalities. Larry was quiet, imaginative, and plodding, but compelling.

North Wake had elders that gave careful oversight to the congregation. I'd never experienced that. The preaching schedule walked through books of the Bible instead of being topically ordered. I'd never experienced that. The church offered small groups, which dove deeper into the sermon passage and then broke into accountability groups where we'd ask one another hard questions and pray for one another. I'd never experienced that.

My wife, Andi, and I slowly came to be known and loved by the members of the church. Before long, our lives were wedded with theirs. People told me that our time in seminary was going to be some of the best years of our lives. They were right, but maybe not for the reasons they expected.

As we leaned into the church community, Andi and I started leading a small group, and I began teaching Sunday school. One of our elders discipled me. As we came to the end of seminary, we started to think about church planting. That's when Jeff Doyle, one of our elders, came to a few of us and informed us that North Wake desired to plant churches. He invited a small group of us into a church-planting residency. We didn't have to pray long. We loved this church and we knew they loved us. Along with another set of brothers, Joey and I put our "yes" on the table.

Churches Planting Churches

Churches plant churches. Since you picked this book up, I assume you already agree with that. But we should think more about this. Parachurch organizations are wonderful. We benefited from and continue to participate in them. But I want to convince you that they're merely supplemental to your understanding of what it means to be "sent out." I'd like to convince you that the preparation and expertise you need can be found right there in the local church.

I've been in DC long enough to see church planters come and go. I've met with brothers here in the city and talked church planting, and it always strikes me as odd when a prospective planter's sending church isn't around. The church doesn't send anyone to look after the planters. More often, these planters find help from parachurch representatives whose job is to make the prospective planter-pastor aware of various local opportunities.

But if churches plant churches, then wouldn't it make the most sense to see more local church pastors walking around a town with a prospective planter than it would be to see them walking around a town with a parachurch representative?

Parachurch ministries are no substitute for the local church. The reason for this is simple. A parachurch ministry sees the best of you for a short amount of time; your local church sees the best *and* the worst of you for the *most* amount of time. In other words, they really know you.

This difference is sort of like the difference between dating and marriage. In dating, you always show up looking your best and on your best behavior. You're easy to like. In marriage, you and your spouse see each other with bedhead and you smell each other without cologne. A person who's been on a few dates with you knows something about you. But no one knows you better than a spouse.

It's one thing to be "sent" and forgotten by a local church. It's another thing entirely to maintain a strong relationship with your sending church even after you plant. By all means, engage useful parachurch ministries. I help lead one! But dance with the one that brought you and knows you best. In other words, be meaningfully evaluated, sent, and sustained by your local church.

The Doctrine and Life of a Planter

In 1 Timothy, the apostle Paul writes to his young disciple, Timothy, who is pastoring a church Paul planted in Ephesus. Paul exhorts Timothy to make sure that "certain people" don't teach false doctrines or promote wrongheaded speculations about the gospel (1 Tim. 1:3–4). This is a serious concern for Paul. After all, he addressed this same thing with the elders of this same church on his final visit with them (Acts 20:17–35).

Toward the end of the letter Paul tells Timothy that he should "practice these things, immerse yourself in them, *so that all may see your progress.* Keep a close watch on yourself and on the teaching" (1 Tim. 4:15–16).

Paul understood that Timothy needed to immerse himself in the truth *in the life of the church.* How else could they see his progress? Together with the church, Timothy needed to keep a close watch on his life and the purity of his doctrine.

Life

When we were going through our church-planting residency, we participated in modules on marriage, suffering, and evangelism, among other things. Not only were we taught these things, but our pastors evaluated our fitness in relation to them.

I sat at Jeff Doyle's dinner table countless times with my wife. Jeff was the pastor in charge of the residency. He didn't just watch me interact with my wife over a long weekend. He watched us up close for over four years. When my three-month-old son's life was hanging in the balance, my church watched me labor under that trial.

There's a danger in those who "profess to know God, but . . . deny him by their works" (Titus 1:16). Think about that well-known incident of Paul and Peter in Galatians. Paul could *see* Peter pulling back from the Gentiles when James and the Jews showed up (Gal. 2:11–14). Paul rebuked Peter "to his face" because Peter's words and actions didn't match.

Peter's statement of beliefs was fine. Had some church-planting strategist (or Paul) asked Peter if he believed that Jews were ethnically superior to Gentiles, he would have strenuously said no! Then he would have talked about his vision of hot dogs and ham sandwiches coming down from the sky (see Acts 10). But Peter needed more than an interview; he needed people in his life who were close enough to see him mess up, whom he trusted enough to listen to their rebuke. We can't all have an apostle on our side, but all of us can have local churches invested with divine authority to encourage and rebuke us.

Doctrine

Any time I taught in North Wake's Sunday school, I had at least two levels of accountability. First, many members of the church were listening in, and the majority of them were equipped to spot error. Second, I was recorded so that any of our elders could listen in and make sure I wasn't teaching something that didn't accord with sound doctrine (Titus 2:1). Thankfully, I don't have any horror stories of false teaching. I did, however, watch other brothers get corrected. It was awkward and painful, but the elders were gentle and loving. Think for a moment about all the churches that were served as a result of the members' and elders' careful correction to those seminarian missteps.

When planters either faintly involve the church or completely bypass meaningful engagement, they risk hurting the very people they hope to serve. To distance yourself from this ministry is to distance yourself from God's good gift to help you in planting a church.

Parachurch ministries will ask you to agree to a statement of beliefs. Perhaps they will ask you a handful of questions and listen to you teach a few times. But none of this can replace the three-dimensional experience of seeing one's life and doctrine up close and personal over the course of time.

Sustainer of the Plant

Not only does the local church serve planting pastors in preparation, but they also serve the church plant once the laborers land on the field.

The first few months of planting can be abstract and undefinable. I mean, what do you *do* on the first day? The first week? We tried to offer clear answers to those questions by creating "weekly priorities" sheets. These sheets included all kinds of things—from evangelistic opportunities to administrative tasks. We'd email that to Jeff back at North Wake; in the early days, we'd have weekly calls. He'd answer questions and pray with us. He'd also admonish us when we were or were not doing something wisely. For instance, I was kindly told to drop one of my activities when he found out I was spending so much time away from the home while Andi stayed back to care for our one-year-old son.

This was really helpful, but the pastors and members of North Wake couldn't stay in touch with us since we were four and a half hours away; besides, they had their own lives and ministries in front of them.

In stepped the leadership of Capitol Hill Baptist. They threw open the coffers and said, "Take anything you want if it will make you fight for the glory of Christ and the good of his church." Mark Dever gave me time. I attended their elder meetings, just to sit on the outside and learn. I was new to preaching, so one of their pastors listened to a few of my sermons and gave me feedback. They gave us money and boxes of books to give away. And this doesn't even scratch the surface. Eventually, they sent their own members to join us. To this day, I don't know if we would still be here if it weren't for Capitol Hill Baptist Church. We often refer to ourselves as her adopted daughter because we were treated like family.

If you're planting a church, prayerfully find a gospel-loving church in the town that will treat you like this. Find a church that will let you heal and rest and who will put tools in your hands and send you back, encouraged.

If you're pastoring a more established church, seek out planters and their teams and find ways to serve them. Don't just think about money. How can you send people and other resources their way? How can you encourage them? How can you multiply their young ministry? Be creative. After all, they're not competition. They're family.

Parachurch ministries can, of course, help with some of this. I could tell you about many people who loved us and served us well—and still do! But as helpful as these folks are, their organizations simply aren't built to do the kind of work that local churches can do. Parachurch organizations are like foster families; they meet a specific need for a specific season of life, usually a particularly difficult one. But local churches are family; they walk with their kids every step of the way, through every season of life.

So utilize the help of parachurch organizations. We did, and we do. But be sent out and sustained by local churches.

Commissioning Sunday

Hanging on the wall in our church office is the picture of our "commissioning." On that day, North Wake commissioned not one, but two sets of planter-pastors. We were going to DC, and another group was going to Tampa, Florida. Looking at that picture brings tears to my eyes. Those people were (and are) our family.

I'm glad I have a picture from that day. I can see Larry Trotter, the "baptist-monk" we like to call him, in the front row. Next to him is Mark Liederbach. He pastored me, taught me in seminary and in his home. Next to them are all of our wives. They're the real yet unheralded heroes of church planting. Behind them is a host of people I know, including Drew Ham, my first community group leader, who still sends me texts to tell me he's praying for me. I could go on and on. Every face in that picture is meaningful to me, Joey, and our wives.

If you are going to plant a church, be sent out by a church, not a parachurch. Jesus designed the church to watch your life and doctrine. Jesus designed her to send you and sustain you by the power of his Spirit. So lean upon the church to lead you and love you as you seek to do the same for others.

8

The Team, Not the Man

The Team of a Planter

IN THOSE EARLY DAYS, before planting Restoration Church, I carried an MP3 recorder to my meetings with a group of five couples who all aspired to plant churches. (It was 2008, and my phone wasn't as smart as it is now.)

It's funny to listen now to those highly idealized conversations about our hopes and expectations. Initially, the five couples thought we might plant a church together. We ended up planting several churches—from Cleveland to Richmond to Boston to Tampa to Denver. All of those churches are still thriving. Praise the Lord!

For all of us, planting alone was never a consideration. The goal of this chapter is to encourage you not to plant alone. For both biblical and practical reasons, pastoring by planting is best done with a team.

Biblical Evidence for Teams

It's not hard to find biblical evidence of teams. Think of Moses and Aaron, or Jonathan and David. But we find the best evidence with the Lord Jesus himself, who never traveled alone and chose twelve disciples early in his ministry. He evidently was close to Mary and Martha as well.

When Jesus sent out his disciples to preach and heal, he sent them in teams of two (Luke 10:1). The disciples learned from their Master and practiced the same. Apart from Philip's special mission in Acts 8, the disciples always advanced the gospel together. Peter preaches on the day of Pentecost "with the eleven" (Acts 2:14). He went to Cornelius with a group of disciples (Acts 10:45). The Holy Spirit told the church in Antioch to "set apart Barnabas and Saul" for the work of planting churches (Acts 13:2). Even the epistles to the Thessalonians are cosigned by Silvanus and Timothy.

Throughout Scripture, the disciples spread the gospel in teams. When we establish a witness for Christ, we do so *with others*.

Practical Reasons for Teams

Let's talk about the practical benefits of planting with a team.

Strengths and Weaknesses

I know I'm riddled with weaknesses. I'm not detail oriented. I'm not administratively gifted. And I lack wisdom on a great deal of subjects. Were it not for Joey and my wife, I'd exhaust folks with new ideas without following up on old ones. Even with the one or two things I might be gifted to do, I need Joey and others to rein in those gifts and sharpen them.

There's immense value in offsetting strengths and weaknesses. No one is omnicompetent, and even our competencies needs accountability and sharpening. Strong at communication? You're likely weak at listening. Strong at administration? You may struggle to see the big picture. A church-planting team will minimize weaknesses and maximize strengths.

Accountability

As I mentioned in the last chapter, partnering churches can help, but they can do only so much from afar. For instance, they can't offer meaningful accountability. Saints nearby can, and should. Joey and I would meet every single week to check in on our souls. "How's your time in God's word and prayer?" "Tell me about your marriage. Are you serving your wife?" "Have you handled your money with integrity this week?" "Have you looked at someone with lust in your heart this past week?" "How have you engaged those far from God?" "Are you keeping Jesus clear in your heart and mind?"

In the work of church planting, we can get so focused on what we need to do that we either neglect our own souls or lose sight of the point of it all. Thus Paul's encouragement to "pay careful attention to yourselves" (Acts 20:28). Planting alone makes this difficult, but planting with a team puts accountability within reach.

Encouragement

It's hard to encourage yourself. But it should be relatively easy to be encouraged by others. How often others have encouraged me. Hearing how others would share the gospel worked as fuel for me. Learning that my teaching helped someone put wind in my sails. In those early days, we did almost everything together—handing out materials at Metro stops, planning our services, and walking and praying through our city. The presence of others made our work lighter and more enjoyable.

For those who are married, planting with a team will inject huge doses of encouragement to your wife. Were it not for Joey's wife,

Page, my wife and I wouldn't be where we are. Page was and still is a tremendous blessing to my wife. I failed miserably in the early days because I would stay out all day and come home to my wife—who knew no one in our new city but who was caring for a small child all by herself—and I wouldn't serve her as I should. Having Joey rebuke me for not living with my wife in an understanding way and Page praying with Andi not only made my marriage healthier, but it also made our church plant healthier. As Hebrews tells us, "Let us consider how to stir up one another to love and good works, not neglecting to meet together, as is the habit of some, but *encouraging one another*, and all the more as you see the Day drawing near" (Heb. 10:24–25).

Boots on the Ground

When you plant with a team, you have more laborers to go out into the harvest. In addition to the four of us, we had two amazing sisters join us a year later. Brandi Harris and Michelle Horton were rock stars. They beat the street and met all kinds of people. They welcomed people who needed Jesus into their home. Between my family, the Crafts, and Brandi and Michelle, six sets of feet spread out in Ward 3 in order to make disciples. Every time we came together to report on our work, we were encouraged. If we'd been alone, that work would have been slower, messier, and more taxing.

How Should You Build Your Team?

The benefits of planting with a team are obvious. But collecting the right team isn't so straightforward. How should you build a team?

Prayer

I cannot overemphasize the importance of prayer in planting a church. Prayer is our lifeline into the throne room of God Almighty who "made from one man every nation of mankind to live on all the face of the earth, having determined allotted periods and the boundaries of their dwelling place" (Acts 17:26). If the Lord has determined when and where people live, then you'd be wise to pray and seek his wisdom. Take the time to ask the Lord not only for people, but for the *right people* who will serve for the right reasons in the right place at the right time over the long haul. Prayer is essential.

Going back to that living room in seminary you might ask, "How did all of you know that it was best to go to different cities and not together?" We received wise counsel from our local churches, and we spent time in self-examination and prolonged prayer.

Theological and Philosophical Agreement

Make sure your team agrees with both your theology and your philosophy of ministry. That means everyone intends to uphold the same statement of faith and church covenant.[1] But it also requires larger conversations about what a church is and how to lead one. Does everyone have the same view of church membership and discipline? Is everyone convinced that the Bible teaches something about congregational authority and pastoral leadership? Do they all prioritize expository preaching, congregational singing, and every-member ministry? How does everyone define "success"— by numbers or by faithfulness? Do they think success can be reverse engineered? Or will everyone rely on the ordinary means of grace set out in Scripture, trusting in God to give the growth?

To be clear, you're not looking for uniformity, but you are looking for unity in the core mission and vision of the church. An easy

---

1   See appendixes 2 and 3 for an example of a Statement of Beliefs and a Church Membership Covenant.

way to vet these things is by painting a picture of what the church would look like in her maturity. If that picture excites the potential team members, then you're on the right track.

Expectations and Roles

Defining the expectations and roles of the team well in advance of planting is critical to success. All too often, team members assume they'll have a particular role. This role is usually clearly defined in their minds, but never spoken about with their mouths. This can cause all kinds of interpersonal tension.

A church-planter friend of mine, Justin, experienced a disruption like this early in the work of his team. They planted as a team, and they were clear that they wanted to plant churches that would plant churches. They even talked about having one of their leaders plant. However, you can imagine the surprise Justin felt when, six months after covenanting as a church, another leader announced his plans to begin working on the next plant. Justin told me, "We worked hard at having the right leaders in the right place on the bus, but we weren't clear about when we were going to put those leaders on the *next* bus." By the grace of God, everyone involved was gracious and they worked through it. They eventually planted that new church, but it took five years. But the lesson stands: prayerfully and clearly discuss the roles and expectations of the team in advance.

Perhaps a brother may have expected to preach more, or a musician thought he was going to have more freedom to choose songs. Perhaps a sister thought you would want her to choose the children's ministry curriculum, or another thought she was going to get more financial help. Ministry is hard, and it's even harder at the beginning. So make sure you have many honest and prayerful conversations about who is going to do what and when and how much for how long.

With God's help, we've done this well. We literally didn't even know Michelle when she emailed that she planned to join us. We shared with her what we expected of her and what she could expect from us. We invited questions. You can do the same.

Start with Your Local Church

Where do you start when it comes to building a team? Start by looking for people in your sending church. You likely already share life together. You probably also already agree about theology and philosophy of ministry. Your sending church also provides a reference point for explaining to people what you hope will look the same and what you hope will look different. And that's definitely a conversation you should have.

Remember, churches plant churches. So look around your sending church when building a team.

Our Team

The 1980s television show *The A-Team* featured a motley collection of dudes who helped innocent people. Hannibal was the leader; Faceman was the enticer; B. A. Baracus was the muscle; and Murdock was the pilot. Building a church-planting team works in the same way. You need each part. One or two faces might be up front more than the others, but you need every part of the body in order to disciple all kinds of people (1 Cor. 12:12–31).

Joey Craft is a five-tool gospel player. He manages the day-to-day logistics needed to make our church function. He's also a gifted preacher, but preaching is draining to him in a way that it's not for me. But if I had to handle a tenth of what Joey does, I'd burn out in a week.

Page, Joey's incredible wife, consistently disciples and helps others bear up under heavy weights. She's been a rock for my wife and family.

Brandi and Michelle model the "undivided devotion" that Paul commends among single people (1 Cor. 7). Their lives would have been more comfortable and less expensive back home in the South. But they came to DC to evangelize the lost, disciple women and children, lead community groups, provide counseling and care, and take on a hundred other roles that we needed to thrive. At every step, they are a joy to plant with and to pastor.

Finally, I can't overstate how crucial my wife has been for our church. When we got married, she didn't know she was marrying a pastor-planter. At the time, I was in a stable job, making good money as a sales manager. She once told me she would never leave the state of Georgia. Yet she not only followed me to seminary in North Carolina and then to DC, she also let me choose our apartment in DC without her seeing it first. (I wouldn't recommend that). She has mothered our sons, evangelized the lost, discipled women, corrected me, loved me, and served the entire church in countless practical ways without grumbling or complaining. My wife is one of my church-planting heroes.

This was our core team. I didn't move here to make a name for Nathan Knight. Our small team wasn't here because they trusted me, the man. We trusted one another and, most of all, we trusted Christ. We all moved here to raise up a witness for him.

We also knew our roles, we understood our expectations, and we worked together for the good of those we served that they might know and enjoy Jesus together in a biblically defined church. And believe it or not, fourteen years later, we're still here, doing the same thing we did when we arrived.

Church planters, it's about Jesus, not you—and you can't do it alone. So go find your own A-Team and watch the Lord work wonders.

9

Needy, Not Hip

The Place of the Planter

BEFORE COMMITTING to planting a church in Washington, DC, we thought it would be wise to talk with a DC pastor, the "Baptist bishop" Mark Dever.

We met at Capitol Hill Baptist Church. Dever asked us questions about who we were, what we had been doing, and what our plans were for planting a church. We expected him to affirm our decision to plant in DC. However, we were sorely disappointed.

After listening closely, Mark listed off cities from Richmond, Virginia, to Providence, Rhode Island, explaining that they were in greater need of a healthy church than DC. Were we sure this was the right place? He concluded by telling us that CHBC would be glad to help if we chose DC. But now I wonder why no one else had challenged our decision.

Mark was making sure we had considered DC in terms of kingdom need. More fundamentally, he was pointing to a principle every planter should be willing to consider early on: Is the place you want to go really the place you're most needed?

The Principle

At the conclusion of Paul's magisterial letter to the church in Rome he makes this perplexing statement: "From Jerusalem and all the way around to Illyricum I have *fulfilled* the ministry of the gospel of Christ; and thus I make it my ambition to preach the gospel, not where Christ has already been named, lest I build on someone else's foundation" (Rom. 15:19–20).

Why would Paul say that he has "fulfilled" the ministry of the gospel from Jerusalem to Illyricum? Surely there were plenty of other cities and towns that needed healthy churches, as well as people who had never heard the gospel.

Paul knew there were now gospel witnesses in those locations to continue that work. There were church-planting churches. Therefore, he pressed on to plant churches in places where Christ had not been named.

When Mark asked us to consider whether DC was really best, he was trying to push our thinking into the mindset of Romans 15:19–20. Had we considered whether we should go to a city with no or very few gospel-loving, Christ-enjoying, mission-minded churches? Quite frankly, I'd never thought that way before. I'd been affected by the call to plant churches in major cities. I assumed Washington was in need. Yet I hadn't thought about the need to plant a church where Christ was either not named, faintly named, or falsely named. When choosing a location, ask yourself if you are reflecting the Romans 15:19–20 mindset.

Calling

Within the first ten minutes of most church planters' testimonies or the first few pages of a book on church planting, the word *called* is bound to appear. If you sign up for a church-planting evaluation, you will inevitably be evaluated on your "calling."

Nelson Searcy reflects this emphasis on calling in his church-planting book *Launch*:

> The majority of church plants fail within the first year because the majority of church planters start churches without a clear calling from God. In order to plant a successful church, you have to *know* that you are called by God. Period. There is no way around this truth. Thriving churches have always been—and will always be—built on a base of personal calling, not personal choice.[1]

Planter-pastors need a "calling" to plant, and they need a "calling" to a particular place. If you don't have this, more than likely you will fail. It's that important.

But how do you know you've been "called" to plant in this or that community? If calling is so important to the well-being of a church plant, one would think that Scripture would provide a clear definition of calling. Good news, it does! Paul prays that the Ephesians would "know what is the hope to which he has *called* you, what are the riches of his glorious inheritance in the saints" (Eph. 1:18). Later, he urges them to "walk in a manner worthy of the calling to which you have been called" (Eph. 4:1). Put simply, he has called us to salvation and to walk in a manner worthy of our salvation.

"But this doesn't have anything to do with choosing to be a church planter or choosing a town!" you might think. Correct!

1 Nelson Searcy, *Launch: Starting a New Church from Scratch* (Grand Rapids, MI: Baker, 2017), 37.

The Bible says little to nothing about the kind of calling Searcy and others emphasize. As we saw in chapter 3, it *does* say a good deal about who's qualified to lead a plant. But there's nothing in Scripture that demands or even assumes we'll be able to identify some subjective call from God to a particular place.

This is great news! It frees us from building the church on a subjective, mysterious "call." Instead, we build the church on the rock of Christ Jesus.

Does God know the number of hairs on your head? Yes. Does God know the number of your days? Yes. Does God know how he intends to use you? Yes. Do you know any of these things in advance? No.

A highly subjective calling won't be sufficient when—and I do mean *when*—things get hard. But you know what is strong enough to stand up under the weight of scrutiny? Your baptism, because it points to the strongest calling that you will ever need—your calling to Christ.

Are you qualified to lead a plant? Do your wife and elders agree? Do you have an interest in planting a church there? Do others believe this is a wise choice? Have you fasted and prayed? Well, then, get to it! Don't feel the need to conjure up some story that will be the basis for your plant. As Bible professor Tom Schreiner often says when summarizing Psalm 37:4: delight yourself in the Lord and then do what you want.

What about Hard Callings?

So if the whole world is a possible place of mission, then how can you know exactly where you need to go? Let's begin with the life you've been given.

Your church believes you're a Christian. They also believe you are qualified to lead a church plant as a pastor. Okay, let's move on to your strengths and weaknesses. These will help whittle down where you might wind up.

Let's ask some questions. Where did you grow up? What are your fears? What are your aspirations? What are the common idols of a particular place? Are you willing to step into that day after day? Do you have any nonnegotiables? That's fine. For instance, I had to be able to see the sky. This is one reason I couldn't see myself planting in Manhattan. I also don't handle cold weather well. How about you? By evaluating your answers, you will clarify potential places for service. Of course, don't forget to seek counsel, analyze actual opportunities, and pray.

Now hold that thought for a second. If we're not careful, we may just wind up choosing a place that's cool and comfortable. Joel Kurz, one of my many church-planting friends whom we met earlier, planted in a hard community in Baltimore. "By following the money," he said, "you can oftentimes follow church planting. If we aren't careful, we might communicate to people that Jesus mainly cares about gentrifying, coffee-drinking communities more than communities where people are suffering."

Taking Joel's words to heart, it's worth asking if we have a category for going somewhere where *we know* it will be hard, but we go because Christ hasn't been named or is being faintly or falsely named.

We work with a family that's planting a church in the Middle East. They didn't have the language, the background, or the culture of the people they're trying to evangelize and disciple. And yet, they wonderfully decided to go there.

Not everyone needs to go to the most difficult communities. There are suffering and spiritually needy people everywhere, from the suburbs of Atlanta to the schemes of Scotland. But we all must be willing to go, not to close our hearts and minds off to places just because we "would never."

Put simply, we should welcome others to evaluate our strengths, weaknesses, qualifications, and experiences. But there's more to say about choosing the "right" place.

Talk to Pastors Before

Over the past fourteen years, I've met a lot of guys who want to plant a church in DC. Almost all of them have done their homework. But they often hear only what they want to hear. This tendency is fed by church-planting organizations that accentuate statistics that make it appear as though the need is greater in a city than it actually is.

For example, "Only 24 percent of people in [insert city] go to church on Sunday morning." Or, "There are only so many churches in [insert city] for every person." But abstract statistics rarely tell the whole story. We need to talk to actual people who live there. When we do, we may be surprised to find that things aren't what they appear.

So if you want to plant a church, talk first to pastors and planter-pastors who already live in the place you want to move to. Let their feedback weigh heavily. Listen to the local church pastors more than the church-planting strategists. Further, talk to gospel-loving pastors and planters from denominations and networks outside of your stream. The Baptist church planters I talk to are often surprised when I share with them about all the good work that Anglicans, Presbyterians, and other denominations are doing. They assume DC is in greater need than it actually is because they followed the statistics about their own Baptist circle of churches.

When you talk to the people in ministry where you hope to end up, ask them about how the work has gone. What's it like raising a family? What common issues do they face in evangelism? What's the camaraderie among the churches like? What are the schools like? Would you recommend a church plant like ours? If so, where in the town? Why? Are there some international communities nearby? Who's pursuing them?

Choose a Neighborhood

People sometimes wind up at our church after trying Capitol Hill Baptist. When they googled how far away their new home was from Capitol Hill, they thought three miles away would be an easy trek. But once they got here, they realized that three miles in the District of Columbia is like twenty-five miles in other towns. When you drive through a town, you may think this community feeds into that community, when it doesn't. Information like this needs to be factored in. After you've decided where to plant a church, peel back the neighborhoods of need and see how those neighborhoods connect to others. It may not be what you think.

We contacted pastors, planters, and strategists in the city from numerous denominations. We asked them where the gaps in the city were. Everyone I asked back in 2008 said they were unaware of anything healthy in upper northwest DC. So when I visited, I didn't look anywhere else.

I drove up Connecticut Avenue, came over Western Avenue, came down Wisconsin Avenue, and turned back up Massachusetts Avenue. I looked at the different church buildings and tried to see what was going on. I talked to people on the ground. In the end, we landed where we are not because *we chose* this part of the city, but because other people told us that this was a place of need.

Preach, Pray, Love, and Stay in That Neighborhood

One of the first people I met after moving to DC was Mike Godzwa. He had been doing campus ministry at American University with Chi Alpha for over a decade. In that time, most other campus ministries had failed. Sitting at the restaurant Booeymonger's and scarfing down a Reuben sandwich, I asked him why he thought his ministry had thrived.

He answered in one word without hesitation: "Proximity. We live right next to the campus and we've stayed here for the long haul, preaching the gospel and loving people. That's it."

Most of my life is within three square miles of my home. I can walk to church, the grocery store, and eighty-seven different Starbucks, as well as where my boys play Little League baseball. Not every town works like that. In fact, most don't. But the Lord has made our ministry more fruitful at least in part because of our proximity to those we're ministering to.

There are things I'd like to change about where we live, but I know that would be true anywhere. But after fourteen years, I do believe we were meant to be here. I didn't know that in advance, but after prayer, wise counsel, and some patient, open-minded investigation of all kinds of people on the ground, I can conclude that I wouldn't want to be anywhere else.

10

Love People, Not Programs

The Mission of the Planter

WE'VE TALKED ABOUT what a church is, what a church does, and how a church planter chooses where to go and whom to take with him. But what happens when a potential church planter becomes an actual church planter? It's time to hit the streets.

We spread out all over Northwest DC and tried to meet as many people as we could. We invited countless people into our home. We didn't know anyone in the city, so the task felt daunting. We prayed and targeted a few key areas, like the local university.

I met a Muslim student named Ahmad, who was married to Aida. We were connected by the university, which had a program for helping international students transition to America. We first met on campus at Christmastime, so he asked about our various traditions, like the lights, decorations, and, of course, Santa Claus. We had a great time, so I invited Ahmad and his family to our home for dinner.

When Aida met our sons, she asked what their names meant. With names like Judah and Elisha, it was an evangelistic softball.

Since they didn't share our Western aversion to talking about religion, we jumped straight into what Christians believe. The night was full of questions and answers and growing understanding. It was the beginning of a friendship that endures to this day.

Ahmad had never been to a Christian worship service before. His first time at our church, he sat attentively throughout the whole service. He came back a handful of times and attended social gatherings, and throughout it all, we continued to share the gospel with him.

The Flow

In the early days of our plant, our church hosted events to get to know people in our community, people like Ahmad and Aida. We hosted block parties. We stood at Metro stations and handed out invitations to our Sunday service and other evangelistic studies. We did a "bag drop," where we went door-to-door to provide food for the poor of our city. We've done a few explicitly evangelistic talks that interacted with atheism and the Christian worldview.

All of these activities were good, but our most effective evangelistic ministry was and remains our members building relationships with the people around them. They used their best tool—their dinner table—with intentionality and love.

When someone showed a spark of interest in Christ, we invited them to Sunday gatherings and sometimes community groups. But we prioritized the former. From the pulpit every week, we explicitly address the lost both in the time of welcome and in the sermon. Even in those awkward early days when we knew all twelve people in the room were Christians, we still addressed non-Christians in order to create the expectation that these gatherings are for non-Christians, too.

Our Sunday gatherings, community groups, and individual discipling relationships, marked by mutual care for one another, made our church compelling. Our love for Christ began to attract lost or wandering sheep. People began to trust in Jesus. Sheep without a shepherd stuck around even though our music and my preaching were bad. Why? Because there was an aroma of the gospel so thick you could taste it. We didn't have any flashy programs. No one was impressed by our simple offerings. But they were impressed by a beautiful Savior who stood at the center and foundation of everything we did.

Reaching the Shores of the Jordan

As people would move through the life of our little church plant, we tried our best to do life with them. As Jesus instructed, we knew that one of our greatest evangelistic tools was our love for one another (John 13:34–35). Seeing those baptismal waters stir was not the end of anything, but the beginning of a lifelong relationship with Christ. Like doting and tender parents, we wanted to walk with others as they learned to walk with Christ.

During this time, I ran into a fellow church planter at a conference. I asked him how the work was going. I could tell he was excited: "Just reached a guy for Christ about two months ago!" "That's great!" I said. "Tell me about it." We gave thanks to God, and then I asked, "So how's he been doing since then?" My friend responded, "Well, uh, I went back a couple of weeks later, and he hasn't had any interest in coming to church. So I don't know."

I'm not sure why this pastor was confident he had "reached" that man. We haven't "reached" people if we don't know where they are or how their walk with Jesus is going. We haven't "reached" others if we failed to grieve with them over the loss of a loved one or weren't present to veer them away from a false teacher.

True Christians endure to the end, and they endure to the end with one another's help, safely protected by membership in a church.

Enduring through the Christian life is hard. In our thirteen years, we've seen almost as many people deny the faith as we've seen disciplined out of the church. About 10 percent of our members live on spiritual ventilators—they're barely hanging on. The rest of us go through the standard ups and downs of life—depression, doubt, devastating news, and so on.

We need each other through the rejoicing and the weeping. We need pastors and other members. Life is too hard, Satan is too powerful, and our own hearts are too sinful to think that event-driven ministry will be enough. Think of Demas or Alexander the coppersmith who abandoned the apostle Paul. We'll face people like that in our churches, too. But we continue to love individual people all the way through life as we teach them to observe all that Jesus commanded (Matt. 28:20). Our plans for "reaching" individual people should reflect this.

Planning Your Work and Working Your Plan

When you land in your community and get to work, you will want to establish a philosophy of ministry and plan for shepherding people.

Philosophy of Ministry

In their book *The Trellis and the Vine*, Colin Marshall and Tony Payne write, "The growth of the gospel happens in the lives of people, not in the structures of the church."[1] Robert Coleman,

---

1 Colin Marshall and Tony Payne, *The Trellis and the Vine: The Ministry Mind-Shift That Changes Everything* (Kingsford, N.S.W.: Matthias Media, 2009), 82.

in his classic *Master Plan of Evangelism*, wrote something similar: "[Christ's] concern was not with programs to reach the multitudes, but with men whom the multitudes would follow."[2]

We knew we wanted a ministry philosophy that had enough structure to support the primary work of disciple-making. We emphasized loving people with the truth through thick and thin. We held up the ministry of the dinner table, the sidewalk, and the coffee shop. We wanted to go out and meet real people where they were and invite them to "take up their cross" and follow Jesus (Luke 14:27).

I call this the ministry of the mundane because it appears so unspectacular. It's more difficult to manage. It's harder to measure and nearly impossible to market. But the ministry of the mundane has withstood the arrows of the evil one. It relieves a church from the burden of being staff heavy. It frees up Christians to do what Jesus called them to do—to go and make disciples. Every gospel-loving person should desire and be able to do that.

Most people have found this model both liberating and, honestly, frustrating and burdensome. It's liberating because you don't have hundreds of things going on all the time, screaming for attention. It's frustrating because people who grew up in programmatic churches have trouble seeing the fruit without all the activity. They think little is going on when in fact plenty is going on. But why burdensome? Because we're calling everyone to make disciples, like Jesus does. He doesn't give passes to first- or second-year disciples. Neither will we. We'll equip and train you. We'll be gentle. But we'll call you to go out and love people and not wait for them to come to you.

2   Robert Emerson Coleman and Billy Graham, *The Master Plan of Evangelism* (Grand Rapids, MI: Revell, 2008), 21.

Structures

Not all structures are bad. In fact, every church needs some structure. In our church, we often talk about three main structures: Sunday gatherings, community groups, and individual discipling relationships.

The Sunday gathering is self-explanatory: we expect members to gather every Sunday if they're in town. Our community groups meet during the week to provide midweek fellowship, Bible study, prayer, accountability, and care.

Discipling relationships exist in a variety of forms. Two people might meet up one early morning to go through a good book. Others might meet every other week and take a walk around the neighborhood and pray with one another. I spend a lot of time on my kids' baseball fields, engaging folks with Christ as well as meeting up with guys regularly in different forms. As Mark Dever and Jamie Dunlop put it, we offer a "regulated free market approach" to ministry.[3] The regulation, of course, belongs to the pastors and elders.

All three structures have easily defined and accessible on-ramps. They facilitate our philosophy of ministry while also making it clear to all Christians: "You can do the work of making disciples!" Structures change as the seasons of a church change. We eventually added a youth group gathering and a comprehensive children's ministry. But even those are built around the main three structures. For example, Ahmad was involved in two of those structures even though he wasn't a Christian. He and I met regularly, and he would occasionally attend the Sunday morning gathering.

---

3 Mark Dever and Jamie Dunlop, *The Compelling Community: Where God's Power Makes a Church Attractive* (Wheaton, IL: Crossway, 2015), 195–97.

Conclusion

We don't do everything right, and I wish we saw more baptisms. We prayerfully preach the gospel every week and call people to faith in Christ, but few respond. Ahmed and Aida, for instance, have never responded in faith to the gospel. I once had a pastoral intern join me when I met with Ahmed, and he asked Ahmed what the gospel was. Ahmed explained it perfectly—better than some Christians I know. And yet he rejects it. I love this man. We've shared a lot of life together. But he remains apart from Christ. It grieves me. Yet I also know the Lord is doing ten thousand things that I cannot presently see and will one day be revealed.

The week following our first dinner meeting, Aida was having lunch with a classmate who mentioned that she and her boyfriend were looking for a church. Aida told her, "I went to dinner with a man who is a pastor, and he seemed to know the Bible. You should try that church." Wonder of wonders, she and her boyfriend came. Better yet, they came back. They were struck by the intentionality of the members, the clarity of the teaching, and the honesty with which people walked with Christ and one another. Hector, the boyfriend, became a Christian. They got married. And both of them eventually joined the church. The woman, Kathryn, now works part time for the church helping disciple women in the church.

Though Ahmad and Aida have yet to come to faith in Christ, God used them to invite another couple whose lives have changed remarkably. Who could have planned that?

Proverbs teaches us that "man plans his ways, but the LORD establishes his steps" (Prov. 16:9). Don't plan to win people with pomp or flash. Don't try to attract people with appearance or programs. Love real people over your dinner table and in the gathering of the saints. Yes, do the best you can with your structures. Strive for undistracting excellence. Get a good website. Be thoughtful about what ministries you have. Those things are helpful. But they pale in comparison to loving people with the truth of the gospel. People need to know and love Jesus.

In everything you do, keep the message of Christ clear and prioritize loving others as Christ loved us. This kind of ministry may not make the headlines here on earth. But I assure you, the angels will sing in heaven.

11

Bricks, Not Straw

The Desire of the Planter

"DO WHAT? Are you serious?"

This is how Joey and my wife responded when I asked them if we should plant another church. We all wanted to plant more churches—eventually. But none of us had considered doing it when we were barely off the runway with our first plant.

But I couldn't shake the idea. I'd overheard a church-planting strategist say something about the need for a Spanish-speaking church in the DC area. With a mixture of naïveté and godly ambition, I thought, "Why don't we do it?"

To be honest, I didn't pray as much as I should have about this. I kept saying to myself, "Why not us? Why not now? All we need is a guy to preach the gospel! We can figure everything else out." You'll notice my assessment didn't square with chapter 8—plant as a team. I was so zealous to get the thing going that I overlooked my own counsel. Thankfully, the Lord would make up for my oversight.

Over time, that "you're crazy" look started to go away. So in our third year, with roughly sixty people and well under 50 percent financial self-sufficiency, we started prayerfully working on a Spanish-speaking church plant, while still learning how to plant a church ourselves.

A Concerning Trend

The emphasis on multiplication in church planting has inspired me to be more fervent in evangelism and more creative in finding ways to get our church more involved in planting churches. At the same time, the emphasis on multiplication unintentionally confuses the *goal* of ministry (trusting and treasuring Christ together) with the *means* (planting more healthy churches).

When size, speed, self-sufficiency, and spread (multiplication) are the markers for success, then we can make an idol out of multiplication. Church planters must be careful about this. The goal is always to shepherd people to trust and treasure Christ. That's what we should aim for and celebrate.

To be clear, this doesn't mean that we shouldn't celebrate church planting. We should. But when we celebrate church planting, we must be clear about *what* we're celebrating. Doing so will focus our energies toward the goal of treasuring Christ together.

The Aim, the Strength, and the Cost of Multiplication

Paul instructs his young pastor-friend, Timothy, in a well-known passage: "You then, my child, be strengthened by the grace that is in Christ Jesus, and what you have heard from me in the presence of many witnesses entrust to faithful men, who will be able to teach others also. Share in suffering as a good soldier of Christ Jesus" (2 Tim. 2:1–3).

Here Paul references the transmission of the gospel to four different people: (1) Paul (2) to Timothy (3) to faithful men (4) to still others. Furthermore, this transmission occurs "by the grace that is in Christ Jesus" as "a good soldier of Christ Jesus." A few verses later he tells Timothy to "remember Jesus Christ" (2 Tim. 2:8). In other words, ministers *of* Christ spread the gospel *by* Christ and *for* Christ. Christ is the means and goal of multiplication.

Also, notice the "then" in 2 Timothy 2:1. Paul had just rehearsed the names of people who either stayed with him or fled (1:15–18). Now at the beginning of chapter 2, he's trying to explain that multiplication involves slow, hard work. There will be casualties of real people with real names and stories. We cannot hurry multiplication.

Put simply, there's no reason to aim for "rapid indigenous church reproduction."[1] There's no reason to obsess over numbers. We want to build our ministries on the rock, not the sand. We cannot plant churches with sticks and straw. The work is too important and too hard. God is too great, and people are in too great a need.

In my own context, I've prayed with many pastor-planters who were hurting because they were sold a bill of goods that didn't match what they saw on the ground. I've seen both new disciples and mature disciples struggle to recover when they see pastor-planters move on to the next thing. Those left behind are often left wondering if their pastors were motivated by the same concern that Jesus had when he implored Peter to "feed" and "tend" his sheep (John 21:15–19). In the dozens of membership interviews I've done, I've often found skepticism in these saints because many of their former pastors were unapproachable or disinterested in their lives, even as they led growing churches.

1   V. David Garrison, *Church Planting Movements: How God Is Redeeming a Lost World* (Midlothian, VA: WIGTake Resources, 2004), 21.

As we emphasize spreading the light of the gospel to every neighbor and nation, we must not aim at speed. We must aim at names—names who will gather and go because they've seen and tasted the love of Christ in the church. We must endeavor to multiply not with sticks and straw, but with people seeking to treasure Christ together in biblically defined churches under the faithful shepherding of biblically qualified men.

Preparing the Church for Multiplication

A pastor's job is to prepare members for multiplication. When people join, explain that your church desires to plant other churches. Then they won't be surprised when it happens. This objective will also shape the way you hire staff, the way you shape your budget, and even the way you teach and disciple.

When we established our budget (we call it our "investment strategy"), a nonnegotiable was that at least 10 percent of our money would support church planting. We did this even while we depended on outside financial help to meet our own budget. We also prayed for church plants in our corporate gatherings and served churches that planted in other places. We took day-long or short-term mission trips to expose our folks to new works. Whenever possible, we pointed out church planting in the Scriptures. We deliberately went through the book of Acts early on in order to bake into our DNA this commitment to plant other churches.

You might establish different practices. Perhaps a community group could transform into a local church across town. Perhaps a small group of people could join another church in another part of your town to help revitalize it. Perhaps a group of people want to move overseas to help with an international church in a needy place. Pray for people to go and labor to raise up a witness to Christ, and give thanks for the opportunity to participate in the wonderful work of entrusting to faithful men those who will teach others also.

Preparing the Pastor-Planter for Multiplication

As your church prepares for multiplication, make sure you're preparing pastor-planters. You'll find them most naturally on your elder board or among young men in the church on their way to being elders. Planting and revitalizing doesn't require bringing people in from the outside. Your best pastor-planters may be sitting right in front of you. Do they aspire? Are they qualified? Are they interested? Train those men up.

If you don't have potential pastor-planters in-house, you can also look at your relational networks that share your convictions. See if your fellow pastors know of someone willing, able, and qualified.

This is how we found the first pastor-planter we sent out of our church. After others recommended him, we spoke to him, his family, and his current church. Those conversations went well, so we invited them to meet our church. Our folks got to meet him in many different environments. They even sat under his teaching for a Bible study. Everything went well, so we made our expectations clear and invited him in.

After identifying a team of pastor-planters, prepare them by running them through some kind of residency. Leaning on Paul's language in 1 Timothy 4:16, we spent most of our time on life and doctrine. We set up studies on theology, missiology, ecclesiology, and pastoral ministry. But just as important, work to integrate the team of planters into the life of the church.

We asked ourselves, How do they relate to others? Are they trying to meet their neighbors who don't know Christ? How do they lead their wives and children? How is their prayer life (see Acts 6:4)?

Are they willing to serve in children's ministry? Do they ever show up early and stay late to do grunt work?

As you watch pastor-planters, get to know them as people, not just future planters. Be patient with them and love them as you would one of your sheep. Have flexibility in your residency, knowing that they may not be ready at the end. Also, you must be willing to potentially say, "No, we don't think you are ready/ qualified to plant this church." Make those expectations clear up front. If you compromise on character, conviction, or capability, then you won't reproduce health.

Continuing Preparation

You've prepared your people, and you've prepared pastor-planters. But the work of preparation doesn't end after the planters have left your church. The work is just beginning. As the sending church, you continue to prepare them for what's yet to come.

The planting team will likely feel alone, even if they planted just five miles away. They've grown accustomed to being surrounded by a community that supported them. Now most of that is gone. The absence of community is difficult for planters.

As you endeavor to plant more churches, make sure to plan for the relationship that will need to continue after the planting team has arrived on the field. Eventually, they'll find their way or have another church nearby to help them find their way. Unless, that is, they are overseas. Then you'll likely need to have a longer ramp of maintaining a meaningful connection.

Iglesia Biblica Sublime Gracia

Alejandro Molero and his family joined us for just over a year before we sent them out to plant a Spanish-speaking church in our city.

Another nearby sister church supplied a qualified man and his wife to help Alejandro. We also sent four members with him, making eight core team members.

On the Sunday we commissioned them, we felt as if we were celebrating a first baby. We were clear-eyed on the goal: to see Spanish speakers treasuring Christ together in a biblically defined church under healthy, qualified pastors. Many of us wept that day because Alejandro, his family, and the others weren't going to plant a Restoration Church franchise. They were family, and they were now leaving to start their own family.

On March 4, 2018, Iglesia Biblica Sublime Gracia covenanted together as a church with twelve members. This group of Venezuelans, Guatemalans, and El Salvadorians came together as an embassy of heaven on earth. They hoped in Christ their Savior, and delighted to sit under the ministry of God's word. That little church has since grown, and they have been serving the Latino poor of their community with the love of Christ. People are coming to faith, marriages are being healed, and hope is being given to fearful immigrants. It's beautiful.

On the evening of the covenanting service, I preached through a translator and called them to do as we had done with them: to make disciples who delight in the supremacy of Jesus Christ and to plant more churches both here and abroad.

In thirteen years of pastoral ministry, I've seen many highs and lows. Without a doubt, the planting of Iglesia Biblica Sublime Gracia is one of the highest highs. To see another life come out of our life is not only personally satisfying; more so, it brings honor, glory, and praise to Christ! He is our true and lasting reward!

We continue to work on planting churches in Central Asia, across the United States, and in Washington, DC. Jesus has purchased his church and he is worthy of all praise and glory (Acts 20:28). So with all diligence, we prayerfully and intentionally raise up teams that will be led by pastor-planters that build churches with bricks, not sticks and straw. I pray you'll join us in this greatest of all endeavors.

Conclusion

Defining "Success"

"WELL DONE, BROTHER. WELL DONE."

We had gathered in a restaurant on a sultry summer day in the heart of DC. Outside, laborers set up fences and hung bunting in preparation for the July 4 celebration. Inside, we were having a celebration of our own. About a dozen men had gathered to celebrate the ministry of one of our planters. It was a wonderful occasion.

Dozens of people walked by without interest as the brothers laughed, prayed, and encouraged this precious man. One by one, they spoke words of heartfelt gratitude for how he had inspired and encouraged them in their own ministry. One documented the brother's biblical fidelity, another his eagerness for evangelism, still another his coffee snobbery, followed by another who testified to this brother's love for the church. Our hearts were as full as our bellies as we rejoiced.

Had you been sitting in the neighboring booth and listened in, I'm confident you would have testified to the success of this man, and you would have been right. True enough, we'd come together for a meal to say goodbye. He and his family were transitioning out of the city. They fell short of the indomitable five-year mark. So in the eyes of some, he'd failed. But in the eyes of God, he had not.

Success

This brother and his family labored hard in the city. They tabled at festivals, they did service projects, they prayer-walked, they handed out materials, they invited neighbors over for meals, and they facilitated services that dripped with the gospel. Some came, but after five years he needed to move on so as to not be the "infidel" that Paul speaks of in 1 Timothy 5:8; he needed to be able to better provide for his family.

Did he fail?

Unequivocally, no! He didn't fail. In fact, I would even say that he succeeded more than some church plants that have grown larger and lasted longer.

Church planters plant churches. Pastors are the leaders of churches, and therefore we plant biblically defined assemblies. We do the work of pastoral ministry so that our people might treasure Christ together. That's the often unheralded yet beautiful definition of "success."

We believe that the Lord in his infinite wisdom used a humble teenage girl from nowhere to give birth to the Redeemer. We believe that Jesus won as the world laughed at his loss. Things may appear to be one thing when they are in fact something else.

Successful church planters are like the successful farmer of Mark 4:26–29. He scatters the seed, and he goes to sleep. He does what? He goes to sleep! "The seed sprouts and grows; he knows not how."

Surely if we were to ask the farmer, "How do plants grow?" the planter would know the answer. But Jesus's point is to highlight the sufficiency of the seed of the word. The seed, like the word, is buried into the soil of the world, and fruit comes in the various places we preach that word. We know not how. We can't predict where. There are no "proven strategies," no books (including this one), no enneagram numbers, no amount of charisma that will automatically produce "success." We succeed when we faithfully spread the seed. After that, we can rest in the sufficiency of that seed to do as it pleases the Lord. Read that again: we planters rest in the sufficiency of Christ and the word as we lovingly and liberally scatter the gospel in our communities. What defines our success? Scattering the seed and sleeping.

Five years have now passed, and Iglesia Biblica Sublime Gracia has continued scattering the seed and slept. They've not only baptized a dozen or more from countries all across Central and South America, but they will soon birth their own church plant. More than a dozen planting-pastors meet in our office each month for prayer, counsel, and encouragement; they are doing the work and the Lord is blessing their labors. The gospel landscape of DC has changed dramatically because of the faithful discipleship of planters descending upon this city. It's happening. God is working. But it's not flashy, predictable, or perhaps even noticeable to the surrounding community. But God sees, God knows, and God remembers. And he is pleased.

Rest well, friends. Go to sleep with joy in your hearts and hope for tomorrow. No matter what comes when the sun rises, you can rest assured that if you're planting a church by faithfully preaching the word and pastoring saints toward treasuring Christ, then you are absolutely succeeding. Well done, brothers and sisters. Keep it up.

Plant by pastoring names, not numbers.

Appendix 1

Covenant Ceremony

IN CHAPTER 4 we talked about covenanting as a church, not launching a crowd or business. One of the most frequent questions I've received over the years is, How did that look? We wanted to communicate that our gathering did not hold the four *s*'s to be our goal for success. We wanted to communicate right from the beginning that we were a biblically defined, Christ-exalting, covenantal body. What would it look like to covenant together as a church and so communicate who we are, why we exist, and what we intend to do?

The order of service (see below) shows how Restoration Church covenanted together as a church on March 28, 2010. I do not think this is the only way to do it, but this is how we sought to communicate to God, one another, and those gathered that we were starting a church for the glory of God and the good of our neighbors.

I do want to note one of my regrets. You'll notice that after the "Welcome & Announcements," the first thing we did was baptize two people. As I mentioned before, we consciously waited to celebrate the ordinances until we were formed as a church. But for pragmatic reasons, we chose to do the baptisms at the beginning of the service instead of waiting for the formation of the church and then facilitating the baptisms. Ideally, I would have done the baptisms after the covenanting and pastoral installation. It's a small thing, but I believe it would have been more instructive to move those pieces.

After singing, the eighteen prospective members were asked by our "grandmother" church's pastor, Bobby Linkous, to stand. We all knew who we were in advance. We all had participated in membership discussions and received affirmations beforehand. The moment had arrived.

Amid the ears of about fifteen others, we read the church covenant aloud to God and one another. Jesus taught that "where two or three are gathered in my name, there am I among them" (Matt. 18:20). We agreed. Bobby then prayed to God, commending this freshly minted church to Christ.

We then sang "In Christ Alone" as a pledge that it is only by Jesus that we could become a church, and ultimately it is for Jesus alone that we exist.

The congregation was then instructed to be seated while Joey and I were asked to remain standing. Remember, we had never been pastors before. In the preceding months we had acted as pastors, but since we hadn't formed as a church and no one had received us as such, we were yet to formally be installed. This was that moment.

You can see the questions that were read to us by brother Bobby as we stood among the congregation. We responded as written. After this, we were asked to be seated as the other newfound members of Restoration Church were asked to stand. They were then asked the questions listed. When they said "we do" and "we will," tears fell from our eyes. Brother Bobby then gave a brief encouragement to us as pastors and the church as a whole.

Appropriately, we sang "O Church Arise," which was followed by a sermon from Jeff Doyle. Preaching from Ephesians 4, he movingly called us to our work as a church. We then celebrated the Lord's Supper together for the first time. Up until this day, we had refrained from celebrating baptism and the Lord's Supper. It was a solemn occasion when the covenant members of this newborn embassy for the kingdom ate and drank together, remembering what made us a people while also anticipating the day when we would eat with Christ together in his consummated kingdom forever, together. The "many" of the prospective members who had become "one body" partook of the "one bread" (1 Cor. 10:17). The church was formed. Glory hallelujah!

After we sang "Jesus, Thank You," Joey offered a final prayer and a benediction.

The members then came up to the front and signed a handwritten copy of the church covenant, which had been contracted to be written on a large sheet in calligraphy. That same document now hangs on a wall, by God's strange providence, just a few feet away from where we signed it in the building that is now our own. Who could have ever thought the meetinghouse we rented for this special service would end up being our home? Only God.

There was no mistaking the purpose of this special church service. It made clear who we were, what we believed, what we were becoming, and why we existed: to treasure Christ together.

Don't make people have to guess what happened on your "launch Sunday." Make the church clear, make it distinct, make it confessional, make it doxological! Covenant together on that Sunday under word and prayer. It won't be flashy, but it will be purposeful, instructive, and compelling.

Order of Service Sunday, March 28, 2010

Welcome & Announcements

Celebration of Baptism

Congregational Singing "And Can It Be?"
"Arise, O God, and Shine"

Covenant Affirmation

Pastoral Prayer

Congregational Singing "In Christ Alone"

Pastoral Installation & Vows

Congregational Encouragement Bobby Linkous

Pastoral Prayer

Congregational Singing "O, Church Arise"

Sermon "Growing Up Together" Ephesians 4:4–16
Jeff Doyle

Celebration of the Lord's Supper

Congregational Singing "Jesus, Thank You"

Reflection Please spend the next few moments silently
reflecting on this evening's service.

Pastoral Vows

Do you reaffirm your faith in Jesus Christ as your own personal Lord and Savior? **I do**.

Do you believe the Scriptures of the Old and New Testaments to be the word of God, totally trustworthy, fully inspired by the Holy Spirit, the supreme, final, and the only infallible rule of faith and practice? **I do**.

Do you sincerely believe the Statement of Faith and Covenant of this church contain the truth taught in the Holy Scriptures? **I do**.

Do you promise that if at any time you find yourself out of accord with any of the statements in the Statement of Faith and Covenant you will on your own initiative make known to the other elders the change which has taken place in your views since your assumption of this vow? **I do**.

Do you promise to submit to your fellow elders in the Lord? **I do, with God's help**.

Have you been induced, as far as you know your own heart, to accept the office of elder from love of God and sincere desire to promote his glory in the gospel of his Son? **I have**.

Do you promise to be zealous and faithful in promoting the truths of the gospel and the purity and peace of the church, whatever persecution or opposition may arise to you on that account? **I do, with God's help**.

Will you be faithful and diligent in the exercise of all your duties as an elder, whether personal or relative, private or public, and will you endeavor by the grace of God to adorn the profession of the gospel in your manner of life, and to walk with exemplary piety before this congregation? **I will, by the grace of God**.

Are you now willing to take personal responsibility in the life of this congregation as an elder to oversee the ministry and resources of the church, and to devote yourself to prayer, the ministry of the word, and the shepherding of God's flock, relying upon the grace of God, in such a way that Restoration Church, and the entire church of Jesus Christ, will be blessed? **I am, with the help of God**.

Congregational Vows

Do you, the members of Restoration Church, acknowledge and publicly receive these men as elders, as a gift of Christ to this church? **We do**.

Will you love them and pray for them in their ministry, and work together with them humbly and cheerfully, that by the grace of God you may accomplish the mission of the church, giving them all due honor and support in their leadership to which the Lord has called them, to the glory and honor of God? **We will**.

Appendix 2

Statement of Beliefs

OUR STATEMENT OF BELIEFS is not meant to be an exhaustive statement of all doctrine, but rather a summary of some essential elements
of the Christian faith laid out in Scripture. It is the affirmation of this
statement that holds our fellowship in unity and guards the purity of
our church. While a full understanding and the ability to adequately
articulate these beliefs is not required, the explicit rejection of any one
of these particular beliefs disqualifies one from membership.

1. The Bible

We believe that the Holy Bible, consisting of the Scriptures of the
Old and New Testaments, alone is the word of God, being fully
written under the inspiration of the Holy Spirit, and therefore is
without error in the original manuscripts and has supreme authority in all matters of faith and conduct. (Ps. 19:7; Isa. 40:8; Mark
13:31; John 20:31; Acts 20:32; 2 Tim. 3:16–17; 2 Pet. 1:20–21)

2. God

We believe that there is one living and true God, the Maker,
Preserver, and Ruler of all things, having in and of himself all

perfections and being infinite in them all. To him all creatures owe the highest love, reverence, trust, and obedience. (Deut. 6:4; Ps. 145:3; John 1:3; Rom. 11:36; 1 Cor. 8:4–6; 10:31; Col. 1:16–17; 1 Tim. 1:17)

3. The Trinity

We believe that God eternally exists in three persons, Father, Son, and Holy Spirit, that these are without division of nature, essence, or being and are equal in every divine perfection. (Gen. 1:1, 26; Matt. 3:16–17; 28:19; John 1:1, 3; 4:24; Rom. 1:19–20; 2 Cor. 13:14; Eph. 4:5–6)

4. God the Father

We believe that God the Father, a personal spirit, infallibly fore-knows all that shall come to pass, including the future free choices of all humans and other moral beings, that he concerns himself mercifully in the affairs of humanity, that he hears and answers prayer, and that he saves from sin and death all who come to him through Jesus Christ. (Matt. 23:9; Luke 10:21–22; John 3:16; 6:27; Rom. 1:7; 1 Tim. 1:1–2; 2:5–6; 1 Pet. 1:3; Rev. 1:6)

5. Jesus Christ

We believe that Jesus Christ is God's only begotten Son and is fully God and fully man. We believe in his virgin conception by the Holy Spirit, sinless life, miracles, and teachings. We believe in his substitutionary atoning death, bodily resurrection, ascension into heaven, perpetual intercession for his people, and personal, visible return to earth. We believe that he is the divinely appointed and only mediator between God and man, the prophet, priest, and king of the church, and Sovereign of the universe. (Isa. 53:10–12; Matt. 1:18–25; 20:28; Luke 1:26–38; John 1:1, 14, 18; 10:30;

17:3; 20:28, 30–31; Acts 1:9–11; 20:28; Rom. 5:6–8; 6:9–10; 8:34; 9:5; 1 Cor. 8:6; 15:3–4; 2 Cor. 5:21; Gal. 3:13; Eph. 1:4; Phil. 2:5–11; Col. 1:15–20; Heb. 1:1–3; 7:25; 9:28; 1 Tim. 2:5; 3:16; Titus 2:13; 1 Pet. 2:21–23; Rev. 12:10)

6. Holy Spirit

We believe in the Holy Spirit who came forth from the Father and Son to convict the world of sin, righteousness, and judgment, and to regenerate, sanctify, and empower all who believe in Jesus Christ. We believe that the Holy Spirit indwells every believer in Christ, and that he is an abiding helper, teacher, and guide. (John 14:16–17, 26; 15:27; 16:9–14; Rom. 8:9, 14–17; 1 Cor. 3:16; 6:19; Gal. 5:22–26; Eph. 1:13–14)

7. Providence

We believe that God from eternity decrees or permits all things that come to pass and perpetually upholds, directs, and governs all creatures and all events, yet so as not in any way to be author or approver of sin nor to destroy the free will and responsibility of moral beings. (Isa. 46:9–11; Prov. 16:33; Col.1:17; Heb. 1:3; James 1:13–15)

8. The Fall of Man

We believe that God originally created man and woman in his own image and free from sin, but they willfully sinned against God and thereby incurred physical, spiritual, and eternal death, which is separation from God, and that, as a consequence, all human beings are born with a nature corrupt and wholly opposed to God and his law, are sinners by choice, and are under condemnation. (Gen. 1:26–27; 2:17; 3:1–7, 19; 6:5, 12; 8:21; Jer. 17:9; John 5:24;

Rom. 3:9–23; 5:12–19; 6:21, 23; 7:13; 8:6–7; 9:22; Eph. 2:1–3; 2 Thess. 1:9; James 1:14–15; 1 John 3:14; Rev. 21:8)

9. Regeneration

We believe regeneration is a change of heart, wrought by the Holy Spirit, who gives life to the dead in trespasses and sins, enlightening their minds spiritually and renewing their whole nature, so that they love and practice holiness. (Ezek. 36:25–26; John 1:13; 3:3, 5–8; 2 Cor. 5:17; Gal. 2:20; Eph. 2:1–6; Titus 3:5; 1 John 5:1)

10. Repentance and Faith

We believe that salvation is conditioned upon genuine repentance and faith, which follow upon God's gracious drawing of sinners through the gospel. Repentance occurs when a person, being by the Holy Spirit made sensible of the manifold evil of his sin, detests and forsakes it, humbling himself with godly sorrow and self-abhorrence, and endeavors to walk before God so as to please him in all things.

Saving faith is the belief, on God's authority, of whatever is revealed in his word concerning Christ and accepting and resting upon him alone for justification and eternal life. It is accompanied by all other saving graces and leads to a life of holiness. (Prov. 28:13; Matt. 3:8–10; Mark 1:15; John 3:16, 36; 5:24; 6:40, 44, 65; Acts 2:37–38; 11:18; 13:38–39; 17:30; 20:21; Rom. 2:4–5; 3:21–28; 4:1–5; 4:17–25; 8:1; 10:3–4, 14, 17; 2 Cor. 5:21; 7:10–11; Eph. 2:8–10; Phil. 1:29; 3:9; Heb. 11:6; James 2:14–26)

11. Justification

We believe justification is God's gracious and full acquittal of sinners, who believe in Christ, from all sin, through the satisfaction that Christ has made, not by anything done by them, but on account of the obedience and satisfaction of Christ, they receive his righteousness by grace alone through faith alone. (John 1:16; Acts 10:43; 13:39; Rom. 3:24–26; 4:23–25; 5:1–21; 8:1; Eph. 2:8–9; Phil. 3:7–9; Titus 3:5–6; 1 John 2:12)

12. Sanctification

We believe that those who have been regenerated are also sanctified by God's word and the indwelling presence and power of the Holy Spirit. This sanctification is progressive through the supply of divine strength, which all saints seek to obtain, pressing after a heavenly life in delightful obedience to all Christ's commands. (John 17:17, 19; Rom. 12:1–2; 15:16; 1 Cor. 1:30; 6:11; 2 Cor. 3:18; Eph. 1:4; Phil. 1:9–11; 2:12–13; 3:12–16; 1 Thess. 4:3; 5:23; Heb. 2:11; 6:1; 10:10; 12:10; 1 Pet. 2:2; 2 Pet.1:5–8; 1 John 2:29)

13. Perseverance of the Saints

We believe that those whom God has accepted in Christ and sanctified by his Spirit will never totally nor finally fall away from the state of grace but shall certainly persevere to the end, and though they may fall, through neglect and temptation, into sin, whereby they grieve the Spirit, impair their graces and comforts, bring reproach on the church and temporal judgments on themselves, yet they shall be renewed again unto repentance and be kept by the power of God through faith unto salvation. (Jer. 32:40; John 8:31; 6:66–69; 10:27–30; Rom. 8:28–39; Eph. 1:11–14; Phil. 1:6; Heb. 13:5; 1 John 2:27–28; 3:9; 5:12, 18)

14. The Church

We believe in the universal church, a living spiritual body of which the Lord Jesus Christ is the head and all regenerated persons are members. We believe in the autonomous local church, consisting of baptized believers in Jesus Christ, who have given a credible profession of faith and have covenanted together for worship, edification, discipline, fellowship, and spreading of the gospel. We believe that the scriptural offices are bishops/pastors/elders and deacons. (John 10:16; Acts 1:8; 2:42–47; 6:1–6; 20:17, 28; Eph. 1:22; 2:19–22; 4:11–16; 5:19–21, 23; Col. 1:18; 3:16; 1 Tim. 3:1–12; Titus 1:5–9; Heb. 3:13; 10:24–25)

15. The Ordinances

We believe that the Lord Jesus Christ has committed two ordinances to the local church, baptism and the Lord's Supper. Baptism is obligatory upon every believer, wherein a person is immersed in water in the name of the Father and of the Son and of the Holy Spirit, as a sign of their fellowship with the death and resurrection of Christ and of remission of sins. We believe that the Lord's Supper is in no sense a sacrifice, but was instituted by Christ to commemorate his death, to confirm the faith and other graces of Christians, and to be a pledge and renewal of their communion with him and with each other. We believe that these two ordinances should be observed and administered until the return of the Lord Jesus Christ. (Matt. 26:26–29; 28:18–20; Acts 2:38; Rom. 6:3–5; 1 Cor. 10:16–17; 11:23–31; 12:13)

16. The Last Things

We believe in the personal and visible return of the Lord Jesus Christ to earth and the establishment of his kingdom. We believe in the resurrection of the body, the final judgment, the eternal joy of the righteous, and the endless suffering of the wicked. (Matt.

16:27; 25:31–46; Mark 14:62; John 5:28–29; 14:3; Acts 1:11; 17:31; Rom. 2:6–11; 1 Cor. 4:5; 15:12–28; 2 Cor. 5:1–10; Phil. 3:20; 1 Thess. 4:15; 2 Tim. 4:1, 8; 2 Thess. 1:7–10; Titus 2:13; Rev. 20:4–6, 11–15)

Appendix 3

Church Membership Covenant

Introduction

Having, as we trust, been brought by divine grace to repent and believe in the Lord Jesus Christ and to give up ourselves to him, and having been baptized upon our profession of faith, in the name of the Father and of the Son and of the Holy Spirit, we do now, relying on his gracious aid, solemnly and joyfully covenant with each other.

Mutual Commitments

We will work and pray for the unity of the Spirit in the bond of peace. (Eph. 4:1–3; Phil. 2:1–4; Col. 3:12–15)

We will walk together in brotherly love, exercise an affectionate care and watchfulness over each other, and faithfully admonish and entreat one another as occasion may require. (Rom. 12:9–16; Gal. 6:1–10; 1 Thess. 5:11–15)

We will gladly cooperate with and submit ourselves to the elders of this church for the care of our souls, which is for our good. (Heb. 13:7, 17)

We will not forsake the assembling of ourselves together, nor neglect to pray for ourselves and others. (Heb.10:24–25; Eph. 6:18; James 5:16)

We will endeavor to raise the children under our care in the nurture and admonition of the Lord, and by a pure and loving example to seek the salvation of our family and friends. (Deut. 6:1–4; Matt. 28:19–20; Eph. 6:1–4; Jude 22–23)

We will rejoice at each other's happiness and endeavor with tenderness and sympathy to bear each other's burdens and sorrows. (Rom. 12:15; 1 Cor. 12:26; Gal. 6:2)

We will seek, by divine aid, to live carefully in the world, denying ungodliness and worldly lusts, and remembering that, as we have been voluntarily buried by baptism and raised again from the symbolic grave, so there is on us a special obligation now to lead a new and holy life. (Rom. 6:4; 12:1–2; Phil. 2:12; 1 Thess. 5:21–22; Titus 2:11–14; 1 Pet. 1:14–16)

We will work together for the continuance of a faithful evangelical ministry in this church, as we sustain its worship, ordinances, discipline, and doctrines. (Phil. 1:27; Jude 3)

We will responsibly steward our spiritual gifts to the service of this church and the community at large. (Rom. 12:3–8; 1 Cor. 12:4–26; Eph. 4:11–16; 1 Pet. 4:10–11)

We will contribute cheerfully and regularly to the support of the ministry, the expenses of the church, the relief of the poor, and the spread of the gospel through all nations. (1 Cor. 16:1–2; 2 Cor. 8:1–3; 9:6–7; Gal. 6:10; 1 Tim. 5:17–18)

We will agree to the Statement of Beliefs and the Restorative Church Discipline policy as defined by this church. (Matt. 18:15–20; 1 Cor. 5:1–12; 2 Tim. 4:2; Jude 3)

We will, when we move from this place, as soon as possible, unite with some other church where we can carry out the spirit of this covenant and the principles of God's word. (Heb. 10:24–25)

Benediction

May the grace of the Lord Jesus Christ and the love of God
and the fellowship of the Holy Spirit be with us all. Amen.

General Index

Aaron, 87
Abraham, 3, 67
accountability, 89
actual belief, 67–70
Addison, Steve, 3
Alexander the coppersmith, 108
alliteration, 79
American University, 77, 104
anger, 39
Anglicans, 102
Antioch, 45
apostles, 44–46
Areopagus, 26
arrogance, 37
aspirations, 101
A-Team, The, 93
atheism, 106
authority, sharing of, 19–20

"bag drop," 106
baptism, 45, 47, 73, 100, 111, 125–26
baptismal, 44
Baptists, 102
belief, 67–70
Bible, 44, 131
Bible studies, 25
Bird, Warren, 3, 6
block parties, 106
boring preaching, 33–34, 41–42
breathing, 73
budget, 116

burdensome, 109
business, 8

calling, 98–100
Calvin, John, 46, 47
capability, 36
Capitol Hill Baptist, 84–85, 97, 103
cause, 59
Chandler, Matt, 34
character, 35, 39, 42
charisma, 34–39, 40, 42
Christian life, 27, 40
Christian worldview, 10, 106
church, 135–36
    definition of, 12, 27, 46–48
    glory of, 53–54
    life of, 82–83
    multiplication of, 116–17
    as planting churches, 80–81
    preaching on, 43
    as sturdy, 20–21
    uniqueness of, 60
church covenant, 48, 91
church discipline, 91
church membership, 31–32, 91,
    139–41
church multiplication movement, 3
church planting
    as an office, 30–31
    vs. pastors, 29–31
    principle of, 98

Scripture Index

 **9Marks**

Building Healthy Churches

9Marks exists to equip church leaders with a biblical vision and practical resources for displaying God's glory to the nations through healthy churches.

To that end, we want to see churches characterized by these nine marks of health:

1. Expositional Preaching
2. Gospel Doctrine
3. A Biblical Understanding of Conversion and Evangelism
4. Biblical Church Membership
5. Biblical Church Discipline
6. A Biblical Concern for Discipleship and Growth
7. Biblical Church Leadership
8. A Biblical Understanding of the Practice of Prayer
9. A Biblical Understanding and Practice of Missions

Find all our Crossway titles and other resources at 9Marks.org.

Also Available from 9Marks

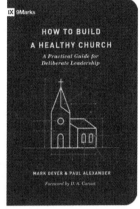

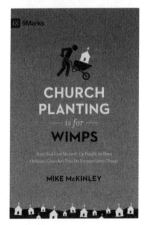

For more information, visit **crossway.org**.